OLD MOORE'S

HOROSCOPE
AND ASTRAL
DIARY

GEMINI

OLD MOORE'S

HOROSCOPE AND ASTRAL DIARY

GEMINI

foulsham

LONDON • NEW YORK • TORONTO • SYDNEY

foulsham

The Publishing House, Bennetts Close,
Cippenham, Slough, Berks SL1 5AP, England

Foulsham books can be found in all good bookshops or direct from
www.foulsham.com

ISBN: 978-0-572-03464-1

Copyright © 2008 W. Foulsham & Co. Ltd.

A CIP record for this book is available from the British Library

Printed in Great Britain by Creative Print and Design Wales, Blaina.

CONTENTS

INTRODUCTION

Welcome to Old Moore's Astral Diaries for the year 2009. Old Moore has been searching the skies on your behalf for centuries now, and the timeless truths of astrology are as relevant to the lives of millions of people today as they ever were. Modern astrology is not seen as a case of each of us waiting around for the forces of the universe to drop good or bad fortune into our laps. On the contrary, it is a complex series of generally subtle changes that have more to do with the way we look at the world and react to it. Astrology gives us an opportunity to make the very best of whatever cosmological forces are acting upon us at any point in time

It is in an effort to harness and use these forces in a positive way that Old Moore has created the Astral Diary for 2009 – a complete book geared specifically towards you and the influences that help to make you what you are.

If you want to know whether a new romance is likely to blossom, if you are in for a good time on the money front or if family concerns could be making you less positive than you might usually be – Old Moore is here to help. The Astral Diary allows you an easy-to-follow, daily account of the way the stars and planets are having a bearing on your life and also lets you know how you can maximise your potential. In addition, the diaries offer space for you to add your own notes and comments.

Old Moore does much more than looking at your zodiac sign because the Astral Diaries let you look much deeper into your own individual nature. What you are as a person is reflected in the time of day you were born and by the position of certain heavenly bodies such as the Moon and the planet Venus. Using unique tables in the Astral Diary you can work out exactly why you are what you are in very specific ways. Once you have this information you can then deal much more effectively with the intricacies of life and will know how to react to both good and not so favourable trends.

Everything you are as an individual is captured within your astrological profile. Using the Astral Diary you can get so close to the core of planetary influence that you can almost feel the subtle undertones that, in the end, have a profound bearing on your life and circumstances. Used in the right way, astrology allows you to maximise your potential, to strike whilst the iron is hot and to live a more contented and successful life. Consulting *Old Moore's Astral Diary* will make you more aware of what really makes you tick and is a fascinating way to register the very heartbeat of the solar system of which we are all a part.

Old Moore extends his customary greeting to all people of the Earth and offers his age-old wishes for a happy and prosperous period ahead.

THE ESSENCE OF GEMINI

Exploring the Personality of Gemini the Twins

(22ND MAY – 21ST JUNE)

What's in a sign?

When working at your best there isn't much doubt that you are one of the most popular people to be found anywhere in the zodiac. Why? Because you are bubbly, charming, full of fun and the perfect companion. But there's more to it than that. Your natural Mercurial charm could coax the birds down from the trees and you exude the sort of self-confidence that would convince almost anyone that you know exactly what you want, and how to go about getting it. Virtually any task you choose to undertake is done in a flash and when at your best you can remove more obstacles than a bulldozer.

So, you ask, if all this is true, why aren't I doing even better in life than I am? The simple fact is that beneath all the bravado and that oh-so-confident exterior is a small child, who is often lost and afraid in a world that can be complicated, large and threatening. If ever there was a person who epitomised a split personality, it surely has to be the typical Gemini subject. That impulsive, driving, Mercury-ruled enthusiasm simply insists on pushing you to the front of any queue, but once you are there the expectations of all those standing behind can begin to prey on your mind. This is why so many of your plans stall before they are brought to completion, and it also explains all those times that you simply run out of energy and virtually collapse into a heap. There is a lot to learn if you want to get the best out of what the zodiac has given you. Fortunately, life itself is your schoolyard and there is plenty you can do to make the very best of your natural talents.

Read through the following sections carefully, and when you have done so, get ready to put all your latent talents to the test. As you grow in confidence, so you will find that you are not as alone as you sometimes think. The keywords for the sign of Gemini are 'I think', but for you this isn't an insular process. Life itself is your launching pad to success and happiness – just as long as you learn to concentrate on the task at hand.

Gemini resources

The part of the zodiac occupied by the sign of Gemini has, for many centuries, been recognised as the home of communication. Almost everything that you are as an individual is associated with your need to keep in constant touch with the world at large. This trait is so marked that Geminis seem to dream more than most other people, so that even in your sleep the need to keep looking, talking and explaining is as essential to you as breathing.

What might be slightly less well understood regarding the sign of the Twins is that you are a natural listener too. One of the reasons for your popularity is that you always seem interested in what those around you have to say. And beneath this desire to know is a latent ability to understand so much about your friends and relatives at an almost instinctive level. Gemini individuals can keep moving forward, even against heavy odds, just as long as a particular project or task feels right, and you should never underestimate the power of your instincts.

The level of your energy, and the way you project it into everything you do, can be inclined to leave others breathless. This is one of your secrets of success because you can be at the winning post so often, whilst others are still putting on their shoes. You are not a trend follower but rather a trendsetter, and no matter if you are on the dance floor of a trendy club, or on a senior citizens' trip to the coast, you are likely to be the centre of attention. The enterprising, interesting Gemini individual skips through life like a barefoot child and elicits just as much joy from those who stand and watch.

Beneath the happy-go-lucky exterior is a great deal more savvy than many astrologers were once willing to grant to the sign of the Twins. However, the advent of the multimedia age has brought Gemini to a society that it not only understands, but in which it excels. On the telephone, the computer and especially the World Wide Web, you spread your sense of fun and offer everyone you meet an invigorating dose of your enthusiasm, knowledge and zest for life.

Beneath the surface

It is likely that most Gemini individuals would consider themselves to be uncomplicated and easy to understand. 'What you see is what you get' seems to be a statement made extremely often by those born under this zodiac sign. It isn't at all true. On the contrary, the Gemini nature is multi-faceted, cranky and often obscure. In short, you have more skins than a Spanish onion. If Geminis have often been referred to as 'superficial' or 'shallow' they probably only have themselves to blame, since they are the first to describe themselves this way. But the truth is that you are a deep thinker – in fact one of the deepest of all. The only reason you don't consider yourself in this light is that your thought processes, like your speech, are lightning fast.

Because of its chatterbox ways, Gemini is often a very misunderstood zodiac sign. But listen to yourself talking. Many of the statements you make to those around you will be ended in questions such as 'Don't you think?'. Why should this be so? Well the fact is that you are never so certain of yourself as you want to give the impression of being, and as a result you invariably seek the confirmation of the world at large that your ideas and plans are sound. If the response you want is late, or not forthcoming at all, you tend to feel insecure and start to fidget. In time this leads to worrying, the worst possible state for the Gemini mind. The dividing line between mental and physical is not at all well defined in your case, so you will often seem most fatigued at those times when you are less than sure of your direction in life.

You almost always start out with the right intentions and would never deliberately hurt another individual. To your very core you are generous and kind. Unfortunately in a busy schedule there isn't always time to let your sensitivity show, and especially not when you live your life constantly in the fast lane. It is almost instinctive for Geminis to divide their lives into 'the job I am doing now', 'the task I will be undertaking in a few minutes' and 'the things I am planning for later'. But even your mind is only capable of so much, so it's essential that you find moments to stop the whirl and buzz of your innermost thoughts. To do so is the hardest task you will undertake, but it's the surest path to health and success that you can ever choose.

Making the best of yourself

It is quite clear that you were never cut out to be a monk or a nun, or at least not of the contemplative sort. Mental desert islands are a natural torture chamber to your zodiac sign and so it's obvious, right from the start, that you need other people just as much as plants need rain. On the other hand, you also need to stop thinking that you can be in control of everything. The hardest lesson for any Gemini to learn is to be selective. Gemini sees life like a wonderfully prepared buffet at which every successive dish offers something absolutely delicious. The idea of trying some of the treats later simply doesn't occur and at the level of daily life the result can often be mental indigestion. Concentration is the key, though without losing the essential freshness and appeal that is the hallmark of your natural personality. 'One job at once' is the best adage, but it doesn't come easy for you.

Your natural talents are suited to intellectual browsing, so you are definitely at your best where flexibility is present. The chances are that you don't really enjoy getting your hands dirty, but even this doesn't really matter as long as you are learning something on the way. You revel in absorbing responsibility and tend to think on your feet. Travel is important to you, not only because it broadens your mind, but also because you are naturally good at languages. You possess a very human touch; you are not frightened to show your emotions and work well alongside others. However, you might function even better if you maintained confidence in your decisions and tried rather less than you sometimes do to be popular with everyone. This comes easier when you are dealing with subject matter that you understand fully, and that in turn takes concentration, which you can only cultivate with practice.

The impressions you give

This section may appeal the most to Gemini subjects because you care deeply about the opinions others have of you. To a certain extent everything you do in a public sense is a sort of performance and just like an actor, you are interested in what the critics have to say. To a great extent you can relax, because there's a good chance that you are much loved. How could it be otherwise? You spread sunshine wherever you go, though it has to be said that you can promote a good deal of confusion too on occasions.

You have to be prepared to take on board the fact that some people will like you more than others do. This is a natural consequence of being such an upfront person. There are people who swim around in the sea of life without making so much as a ripple, but you are definitely not one of them. Some of the individuals you meet will simply not be turned on by the gregarious, enthusiastic, go-getting creature that you are. Once you understand this fact, and stop trying to force your attentions in the wrong direction, your life will be happier as a result.

Another way that you can help yourself is to cultivate humility. Gemini people know at least something about almost everything but there is truth in the adage that 'a little knowledge can be a dangerous thing'. The most successful of those born under the sign of the Twins have learned to defer to experts, most of whom don't take kindly to criticism. You can still maintain your own opinions, but a quiet self-assurance will win you more friends than forcing half-formed opinions on the world at large. On the whole though, you can relax because you are almost certainly more popular than you think you are.

The way forward

Age matters less to Gemini than it does to any other zodiac sign. The fact is that you are always young in your head, no matter how much some of your joints might creak. But even in a physical sense it is important to look after yourself and to recognise those areas that need the most attention. Gemini rules the chest, and especially the lungs, so you should never be a smoker. The sign is also related to the general nervous system, which is almost always pushed to the edge in your frantic attempts to get just as much out of life as possible. Relaxation is just as important as physical exercise, and since you naturally love words, reading is as good as anything. All the same, you shouldn't be constantly trying to learn something, and need to understand that entertainment for its own sake is often enough.

No matter how much your mind wanders, you need to be master of at least one subject – this is the way to success in a professional sense. Whatever your job (and Gemini people are rarely out of work) you will nearly always find yourself in charge of others. Use all the natural understanding that lies at the centre of your being to understand how others tick and you are almost certain to prosper.

On the way through life, professional or social, you can't avoid dealing in gossip, because this is an essential part of the way you function. Casual contacts are inevitable, so you may have hundreds of acquaintances but only a few very close personal friends. However, when you do find yourself absolutely on the same wavelength as another individual, it can be the most enlightening experience imaginable. Geminis often find themselves involved in more than one deep, romantic attachment in their lives, though this is far less likely if your partner is also your best friend.

Don't give in to self-doubt, but at the same time avoid like the plague giving the impression that you know everything. Cultivate patience and spend at least a few minutes each day doing absolutely nothing. Overall, balance is essential, and that isn't always easy to achieve when tottering along the tightrope of life. All the same, a Gemini who is at ease with him- or herself excels socially and grows wiser with every passing day.

GEMINI ON THE CUSP

Old Moore is often asked how astrological profiles are altered for those people born at either the beginning or the end of a zodiac sign, or, more properly, on the cusps of a sign. In the case of Gemini this would be on the 22nd of May and for two or three days after, and similarly at the end of the sign, probably from the 19th to the 21st of June. In this year's Astral Diaries, once again, Old Moore sets out to explain the differences regarding cuspid signs.

The Taurus Cusp – May 22nd to May 25th

It would be fair to suggest that Gemini tends to predominate over almost any zodiac sign with which it is associated so that the trends of this most capricious and gregarious sign tend to show out well at both cusps. Heavily affected by Taurus, however, you are likely to be steadier and more willing to take your time over important matters. Staying power is better and the Taurean cusp inspires a quiet confidence on occasions that seems to contrast sharply with the more chatty qualities of the Twins. Entrenched attitudes are certainly more likely, with a need to prove a point and to seek objectives through determined effort. Taurus here does little to stem the generally cheerful qualities of Gemini but there is likely to be a more serious side to the nature and a willingness to exhibit the sort of patience that is often lacking in the Sun sign of Gemini.

In matters of love, you are more likely than most Geminis to show a high degree of constancy, even if settling on a partner is a longer process in your case. You can't be detached from relationships in the way that the dyed-in-the-wool Gemini can and it's important for you to know that you are loved. Professionally speaking, you have much going for you because in addition to the 'get ahead at any cost' quality that comes from the direction of the Twins, you are persevering, honourable, steadfast and reliable. It is probably in matters of business that the most positive qualities of this astrological matching are to be seen.

Health matters are also stabilised to a great extent on this cusp, partly because the nature is not half as nervy, and more care is taken to get the level of rest and relaxation that is just as important to Gemini. Less rush and push is evident, though a need for change and diversity probably won't be eradicated from your basic nature. There is a good chance that you are something of a home bird, at least most of the time, and family matters are often paramount in your mind. Probably the most noticeable trait is your tendency to be more tidy than the orthodox Gemini – which some would say is no bad thing.

The Cancer Cusp – June 19th to June 21st

It could be that the gradual slip from the sign of Gemini to that of Cancer is slightly less well defined than is the case for Taurus and Gemini. However, when working as stereotypes Gemini and Cancer are radically different sorts of signs. Gemini seeks to intellectualise everything, so its catch phrase is 'I think', while Cancer's is 'I feel'. What we would therefore expect, in this case, is a gradually quieter and less fickle nature as the Sun climbs closer to Cancer. You are likely to show more genuine consideration for other people. Actually this is something of a misnomer because Gemini people are very caring too, it's simply a matter of you showing the tendency more, and you are certainly more tied to home and family than any true Gemini would be. A quiet perseverance typifies your individual nature and you are quite prepared to wait for your objectives to mature, which the Twins are less likely to do. Comfort and security are important to you, though, apparently paradoxically, you are a great traveller and love to see fresh fields and pastures new. Given the opportunity you could even find yourself living in some far, distant land.

In affairs of the heart, you are clearly more steadfast than Gemini and love to be loved. The difference here is that Gemini wants to be liked by everyone, but will quickly move on in cases where this proves to be difficult. You, on the other hand, would take any sort of rebuff as a personal insult and would work hard to reverse the situation. Confidence may not be your middle name, but you are supported by the Gemini ability to bluff your way through when necessary, even if the motivation involved is of a more consistent nature.

You may well be a person who has to rest in order to recharge batteries that sometimes run quite low. Your nervous system may not be all that strong on occasions and this fact could manifest itself in the form of stomach troubles of one sort or another. Common sense counts when it comes to looking after yourself and that's something that the sign of Cancer does possess. Whether you are often truly satisfied with yourself and your own efforts may sometimes be in doubt.

GEMINI AND ITS ASCENDANTS

The nature of every individual on the planet is composed of the rich variety of zodiac signs and planetary positions that were present at the time of their birth. Your Sun sign, which in your case is Gemini, is one of the many factors when it comes to assessing the unique person you are. Probably the most important consideration, other than your Sun sign, is to establish the zodiac sign that was rising over the eastern horizon at the time that you were born. This is your Ascending or Rising sign. Most popular astrology fails to take account of the Ascendant, and yet its importance remains with you from the very moment of your birth, through every day of your life. The Ascendant is evident in the way you approach the world, and so, when meeting a person for the first time, it is this astrological influence that you are most likely to notice first. Our Ascending sign essentially represents what we appear to be, while the Sun sign is what we feel inside ourselves.

The Ascendant also has the potential for modifying our overall nature. For example, if you were born at a time of day when Gemini was passing over the eastern horizon (this would be around the time of dawn) then you would be classed as a double Gemini. As such, you would typify this zodiac sign, both internally and in your dealings with others. However, if your Ascendant sign turned out to be a Water sign, such as Pisces, there would be a profound alteration of nature, away from the expected qualities of Gemini.

One of the reasons why popular astrology often ignores the Ascendant is that it has always been rather difficult to establish. Old Moore has found a way to make this possible by devising an easy-to-use table, which you will find on page 158 of this book. Using this, you can establish your Ascendant sign at a glance. You will need to know your rough time of birth, then it is simply a case of following the instructions.

For those readers who have no idea of their time of birth it might be worth allowing a good friend, or perhaps your partner, to read through the section that follows this introduction. Someone who deals with you on a regular basis may easily discover your Ascending sign, even though you could have some difficulty establishing it for yourself. A good understanding of this component of your nature is essential if you want to be aware of that 'other person' who is responsible for the way you make contact with the world at large. Your Sun sign, Ascendant sign, and the other pointers in this book will, together, allow you a far better understanding of what makes you tick as an individual. Peeling back the different layers of your astrological make-up can be an enlightening experience, and the Ascendant may represent one of the most important layers of all.

Gemini with Gemini Ascendant

You are one of the most fun-loving characters in the zodiac, with a great sense of humour and the ability to sell refrigerators to Eskimos. Most people would think that you have nerves of steel and that there is nothing that lies beyond the scope of your ready wit and silver tongue. Unfortunately it isn't quite as simple as this because you bruise easily, especially when you discover that someone is not as fond of you as they might be. Routines get on your nerves and you need as much change and diversity as life will allow. You are the life and soul of any party that is going on in your vicinity, and you have the ability to mix business and pleasure so should get on well as a result.

In love you tend to be rather fickle and the double Gemini is inclined to dodge from relationship to relationship in pursuit of something that remains rather difficult to define. There are occasions when your life lacks stability and this can be provided by the right sort of personal attachment, assuming you manage to find it eventually. It is clear that you are not the easiest person to understand, even though you probably think that you do not have a complicated bone in your body. Most important of all, you have many, many friends, and this will be the case all your life.

Gemini with Cancer Ascendant

Many astrologers would say that this is a happy combination because some of the more flighty qualities of Gemini are somewhat modified by the steady influence of Cancer the Crab. To all intents and purposes you show the friendly and gregarious qualities of Gemini, but there is a thoughtful and even sometimes a serious quality that would not be present in the double Gemini example above. Looking after people is high on your list of priorities and you do this most of the time. This is made possible because you have greater staying power than Gemini is usually said to possess and you can easily see fairly complicated situations through to their conclusion without becoming bored on the way.

The chances are that you will have many friends and that these people show great concern for your well-being, because you choose them carefully and show them a great deal of consideration. However, you will still be on the receiving end of gossip on occasions, and need to treat such situations with a healthy pinch of salt. Like all Geminis, your nervous system is not as strong as you would wish to believe and family pressures in particular can put great strain on you. Activities of all kinds take your fancy and many people with this combination are attracted to sailing or wind surfing.

15

Gemini with Leo Ascendant

Many Gemini people think about doing great things, whilst those who enjoy a Leo Ascendant do much more than simply think. You are the truly intrepid Gemini but you always keep a sense of humour and are especially good to be around. Bold and quite fearless, you are inclined to go where nobody has gone before, no matter if this is into a precarious business venture or up a mountain that has not been previously climbed. It is people such as you who first explored the world and you love to know what lies around the next corner and over the far hill.

Kind and loving, you are especially loyal to your friends and would do almost anything on their behalf. As a result they show the greatest concern for you too. However, there are times when the cat walks alone and you are probably better at being on your own than would often be the case for the typical Gemini subject. In many ways you are fairly self-contained and don't tend to get bored too much unless you are forced to do the same things time and time again. You have a great sense of fun, can talk to anyone and usually greet the world with a big smile.

Gemini with Virgo Ascendant

A Virgo Ascendant means that you are ruled by Mercury, both through your Sun sign and through the sign that was rising at the time of your birth. This means that words are your basic tools in life and you use them to the full. Some writers have this combination because even speaking to people virtually all the time is not enough. Although you have many friends, you are fairly high-minded which means that you can make enemies too. The fact is that people either care very much for you, or else they don't like you at all. This can be difficult for you to come to terms with because you don't really set out to cause friction – it often simply attracts itself to you.

Although you love to travel, home is important too. There is a basic insecurity in your nature that comes about as a result of an overdose of Mercury, which makes you nervy and sometimes far less confident than anyone would guess. Success in your life may be slower arriving with this combination because you are determined to achieve your objectives on your own terms and this can take time. Always a contradiction, often a puzzle to others, your ultimate happiness in life is directly proportional to the effort you put in, though this should not mean wearing yourself out on the way.

GEMINI AND ITS ASCENDANTS

Gemini with Libra Ascendant

What a happy-go-lucky soul you are, and how popular you tend to be with those around you. Libra is, like Gemini, an Air sign and this means that you are the communicator par excellence, even by Gemini standards. It can sometimes be difficult for you to make up your mind about things because Libra does not exactly aid this process, and especially not when it is allied to Mercurial Gemini. Frequent periods of deep thought are necessary and meditation would do you a great deal of good. All the same, although you might sometimes be rather unsure of yourself, you are rarely without a certain balance. Clean and tidy surroundings suit you the best, though this is far from easy to achieve because you are invariably dashing off to some place or other, so you really need someone to sort things out in your absence.

The most important fact of all is that you are much loved by your friends, of which there are likely to be very many. Because you are so willing to help them out, in return they are usually there when it matters and they would probably go to almost any length on your behalf. You exhibit a fine sense of justice and will usually back those in trouble. Charities tend to be attractive to you and you do much on behalf of those who live on the fringes of society or people who are truly alone.

Gemini with Scorpio Ascendant

What you are and what you appear to be can be two entirely different things with this combination. Although you appear to be every bit as chatty and even as flighty as Gemini tends to be, nothing could be further from the truth. In reality you have many deep and penetrating insights, all of which are geared towards sorting out potential problems before they come along. Few people would have the ability to pull the wool over your eyes and you show a much more astute face to the world than is often the case for Gemini taken on its own. The level of your confidence, although not earth-shattering, is much greater with this combination, and you would not be thwarted once you had made up your mind.

There is a slight danger here however because Gemini is always inclined to nerve problems of one sort or another. In the main these are slight and fleeting, though the presence of Scorpio can intensify reactions and heighten the possibility of depression, which would not be at all fortunate. The best way round this potential problem is to have a wealth of friends, plenty to do and the sort of variety in your life that suits your Mercury ruler. Financial success is not too difficult to achieve with this combination, mainly because you can easily earn money and then have a natural ability to hold on to it.

Gemini with Sagittarius Ascendant

'Tomorrow is another day!' This is your belief and you stick to it. There isn't a brighter or more optimistic soul to be found than you and almost everyone you come into contact with is touched by the fact. Dashing about from one place to another, you manage to get more things done in one day than most other people would achieve in a week. Of course this explains why you are so likely to wear yourself out, and it means that frequent periods of absolute rest are necessary if you are to remain truly healthy and happy. Sagittarius makes you brave and sometimes a little headstrong, so you need to curb your natural enthusiasms now and again, whilst you stop to think about the consequences of some of your actions.

It's not really certain if you do 'think' in the accepted sense of the word, because the lightning qualities of both these signs mean that your reactions are second to none. However, you are not indestructible and you put far more pressure on yourself than would often be sensible. Routines are not your thing at all and many of you manage to hold down two or more jobs at once. It might be an idea to stop and smell the flowers on the way and you could certainly do with putting your feet up much more than you do. However, you probably won't even have read this far into the passage because you will almost certainly have something far more important to do!

Gemini with Capricorn Ascendant

A much more careful and considered combination is evident here. You still have the friendly and chatty qualities of Gemini, though you also possess an astute, clever and deep-thinking quality which can really add bite to the Mercurial aspects of your nature. Although you rarely seem to take yourself or anyone else all that seriously, in reality you are not easily fooled and usually know the direction in which you are heading. The practical application of your thought processes matter to you and you always give of your best, especially in any professional situation. This combination provides the very best business mind that any Gemini could have and, unlike other versions of the sign, you are willing to allow matters to mature. This quality cannot be overstated, and leads to a form of ultimate achievement that many other Geminis would only guess at.

Family matters are important to you and your home is a special place of retreat, even though you are also willing to get out and meet the world, which is the prerogative of all Gemini types. There are times when you genuinely wish to remain quiet, and when such times arise you may need to explain the situation to some of the bemused people surrounding you. Above all you look towards material gain, though without ever losing your sense of humour.

Gemini with Aquarius Ascendant

If you were around in the 1960s there is every chance that you were the first to go around with flowers in your hair. You are unconventional, original, quirky and entertaining. Few people would fail to notice your presence and you take life as it comes, even though on most occasions you are firmly in the driving seat. In all probability you care very much about the planet on which you live and the people with whom you share it. Not everyone understands you, but that does not really matter, for you have more than enough communication skills to put your message across intact. You should avoid wearing yourself out by worrying about things that you cannot control and you definitely gain from taking time out to meditate. However, whether or not you allow yourself that luxury remains to be seen.

If you are not the most communicative form of Gemini subject then you must come a close second. Despite this fact, much of what you have to say makes real sense and you revel in the company of interesting, intelligent and stimulating people, whose opinions on a host of matters will add to your own considerations. You are a true original in every sense of the word and the mere fact of your presence in the world is bound to add to the enjoyment of life experienced by the many people with whom you make contact in your daily life.

Gemini with Pisces Ascendant

There is great duality inherent with this combination, and sometimes this can cause a few problems. Part of the trouble stems from the fact that you often fail to realise what you want from life and you could also be accused of failing to take the time out to think things through carefully enough. You are reactive, and although you have every bit of the natural charm that typifies the sign of Gemini, you are more prone to periods of self-doubt and confusion. However, you should not allow these facts to get you down too much because you are also genuinely loved and have a tremendous capacity to look after others, a factor which is more important to you than any other. It's true that personal relationships can sometimes be a cause of difficulty for you, partly because your constant need to know what makes other people tick could drive them up the wall. Accepting people at face value seems to be the best key to happiness of a personal sort and there are occasions when your very real and natural intuition has to be put on hold.

It's likely that you are an original, particularly in the way you dress. An early rebellious stage often gives way to a more comfortable form of eccentricity. When you are at your best just about everyone adores you.

Gemini with Aries Ascendant

A fairly jolly combination this, though by no means easy for others to come to terms with. You fly about from pillar to post and rarely stop long enough to take a breath. Admittedly this suits your own needs very well, but it can be a source of some disquiet to those around you, since they may not possess your energy or motivation. Those who know you well are deeply in awe of your capacity to keep going long after almost everyone else would have given up and gone home, though this quality is not always wonderful, because it means that you put more pressure on your nervous system than just about any other astrological combination. You need to be mindful of your nervous system, which responds to the erratic, Mercurial quality of Gemini. Problems only really arise when the Aries part of you makes demands that the Gemini component finds difficult to deal with. There are paradoxes galore here and some of them need sorting out if you are ever fully to understand yourself, or are to be in a position when others know what makes you tick.

In relationships you might be a little fickle, but you are a veritable charmer and never stuck for the right words, no matter who you are dealing with. Your tenacity knows no bounds, though perhaps it should!

Gemini with Taurus Ascendant

This is a generally happy combination which finds you better able to externalise the cultured and creative qualities that are inherent in your Taurean side. You love to be around interesting and stimulating people and tend to be just as talkative as the typical Gemini is expected to be. The reason why Gemini helps here is because it lightens the load somewhat. Taurus is not the most introspective sign of the zodiac, but it does have some of that quality, and a Gemini Sun allows you to speak your mind more freely and, as a result, to know yourself better too.

Although your mind tends to be fairly logical, you also enjoy flashes of insight that can cause you to behave in a less rational way from time to time. This is probably no bad thing because life will never be boring with you around. You try to convince yourself that you take on board all the many and varied opinions that come back at you from others, though there is a slight danger of intellectual snobbery if the responses you get are not the expected ones. You particularly like clean houses, funny people and probably fast cars. Financial rewards can come thick and fast to the Taurus-Ascendant Gemini when the logical but still inspirational mind is firmly harnessed to practical matters.

THE MOON AND THE PART IT PLAYS IN YOUR LIFE

In astrology the Moon is probably the single most important heavenly body after the Sun. Its unique position, as partner to the Earth on its journey around the solar system, means that the Moon appears to pass through the signs of the zodiac extremely quickly. The zodiac position of the Moon at the time of your birth plays a great part in personal character and is especially significant in the build-up of your emotional nature.

Sun Moon Cycles

The first lunar cycle deals with the part the position of the Moon plays relative to your Sun sign. I have made the fluctuations of this pattern easy for you to understand by means of a simple cyclic graph. It appears on the first page of each 'Your Month At A Glance', under the title 'Highs and Lows'. The graph displays the lunar cycle and you will soon learn to understand how its movements have a bearing on your level of energy and your abilities.

Your Own Moon Sign

Discovering the position of the Moon at the time of your birth has always been notoriously difficult because tracking the complex zodiac positions of the Moon is not easy. This process has been reduced to three simple stages with Old Moore's unique Lunar Tables. A breakdown of the Moon's zodiac positions can be found from page 25 onwards, so that once you know what your Moon Sign is, you can see what part this plays in the overall build-up of your personal character.

If you follow the instructions on the next page you will soon be able to work out exactly what zodiac sign the Moon occupied on the day that you were born and you can then go on to compare the reading for this position with those of your Sun sign and your Ascendant. It is partly the comparison between these three important positions that goes towards making you the unique individual you are.

HOW TO DISCOVER YOUR MOON SIGN

This is a three-stage process. You may need a pen and a piece of paper but if you follow the instructions below the process should only take a minute or so.

STAGE 1 First of all you need to know the Moon Age at the time of your birth. If you look at Moon Table 1, on page 23, you will find all the years between 1911 and 2009 down the left side. Find the year of your birth and then trace across to the right to the month of your birth. Where the two intersect you will find a number. This is the date of the New Moon in the month that you were born. You now need to count forward the number of days between the New Moon and your own birthday. For example, if the New Moon in the month of your birth was shown as being the 6th and you were born on the 20th, your Moon Age Day would be 14. If the New Moon in the month of your birth came after your birthday, you need to count forward from the New Moon in the previous month. Whatever the result, jot this number down so that you do not forget it.

STAGE 2 Take a look at Moon Table 2 on page 24. Down the left hand column look for the date of your birth. Now trace across to the month of your birth. Where the two meet you will find a letter. Copy this letter down alongside your Moon Age Day.

STAGE 3 Moon Table 3 on page 24 will supply you with the zodiac sign the Moon occupied on the day of your birth. Look for your Moon Age Day down the left hand column and then for the letter you found in Stage 2. Where the two converge you will find a zodiac sign and this is the sign occupied by the Moon on the day that you were born.

Your Zodiac Moon Sign Explained

You will find a profile of all zodiac Moon Signs on pages 25 to 28, showing in yet another way how astrology helps to make you into the individual that you are. In each daily entry of the Astral Diary you can find the zodiac position of the Moon for every day of the year. This also allows you to discover your lunar birthdays. Since the Moon passes through all the signs of the zodiac in about a month, you can expect something like twelve lunar birthdays each year. At these times you are likely to be emotionally steady and able to make the sort of decisions that have real, lasting value.

MOON TABLE 1

YEAR	APR	MAY	JUN	YEAR	APR	MAY	JUN	YEAR	APR	MAY	JUN
1911	28	28	26	1944	22	22	20	1977	18	18	16
1912	18	17	16	1945	12	11	10	1978	7	7	5
1913	6	5	4	1946	2	1/30	29	1979	26	26	24
1914	24	24	23	1947	20	19	18	1980	15	14	13
1915	13	13	12	1948	9	9	7	1981	4	4	2
1916	3	2	1/30	1949	28	27	26	1982	23	21	20
1917	22	20	19	1950	17	17	15	1983	13	12	11
1918	11	10	8	1951	6	6	4	1984	1	1/30	29
1919	30	29	27	1952	24	23	22	1985	20	19	18
1920	18	18	16	1953	13	13	11	1986	9	8	7
1921	8	7	6	1954	3	2	1/30	1987	28	27	26
1922	27	26	25	1955	22	21	20	1988	16	15	14
1923	16	15	14	1956	11	10	8	1989	6	5	3
1924	4	3	2	1957	29	29	27	1990	25	24	22
1925	23	22	21	1958	19	18	17	1991	13	13	11
1926	12	11	10	1959	8	7	6	1992	3	2	1/30
1927	2	1/30	29	1960	26	26	24	1993	22	21	20
1928	20	19	18	1961	15	14	13	1994	11	10	9
1929	9	9	7	1962	5	4	2	1995	30	29	27
1930	28	28	26	1963	23	23	21	1996	18	18	17
1931	18	17	16	1964	12	11	10	1997	7	6	5
1932	6	5	4	1965	1	1/30	29	1998	26	25	24
1933	24	24	23	1966	20	19	18	1999	16	15	13
1934	13	13	12	1967	9	8	7	2000	4	4	2
1935	3	2	1/30	1968	28	27	26	2001	23	23	21
1936	21	20	19	1969	16	15	14	2002	12	12	10
1937	12	10	8	1970	6	6	4	2003	1	1/30	29
1938	30	29	27	1971	25	24	22	2004	18	16	15
1939	19	19	17	1972	13	13	11	2005	8	8	6
1940	7	7	6	1973	3	2	1/30	2006	27	27	26
1941	26	26	24	1974	22	21	20	2007	17	17	15
1942	15	15	13	1975	11	11	9	2008	6	5	4
1943	4	4	2	1976	29	29	27	2009	26	25	23

TABLE 2

DAY	MAY	JUN
1	M	O
2	M	P
3	M	P
4	M	P
5	M	P
6	M	P
7	M	P
8	M	P
9	M	P
10	M	P
11	M	P
12	N	Q
13	N	Q
14	N	Q
15	N	Q
16	N	Q
17	N	Q
18	N	Q
19	N	Q
20	N	Q
21	N	Q
22	O	R
23	O	R
24	O	R
25	O	R
26	O	R
27	O	R
28	O	R
29	O	R
30	O	R
31	O	–

MOON TABLE 3

M/D	M	N	O	P	Q	R	S
0	TA	GE	GE	GE	CA	CA	CA
1	GE	GE	GE	CA	CA	CA	LE
2	GE	GE	CA	CA	CA	LE	LE
3	GE	CA	CA	CA	LE	LE	LE
4	CA	CA	CA	LE	LE	LE	VI
5	CA	LE	LE	LE	VI	VI	VI
6	LE	LE	LE	VI	VI	VI	LI
7	LE	LE	VI	VI	VI	LI	LI
8	LE	VI	VI	VI	LI	LI	LI
9	VI	VI	VI	LI	LI	SC	SC
10	VI	LI	LI	LI	SC	SC	SC
11	LI	LI	SC	SC	SC	SA	SA
12	LI	LI	SC	SC	SA	SA	SA
13	LI	SC	SC	SC	SA	SA	SA
14	LI	SC	SC	SA	SA	SA	CP
15	SC	SA	SA	SA	CP	CP	CP
16	SC	SA	SA	CP	CP	CP	AQ
17	SA	SA	CP	CP	CP	AQ	AQ
18	SA	CP	CP	CP	AQ	AQ	AQ
19	SA	CP	CP	AQ	AQ	AQ	PI
20	CP	AQ	AQ	AQ	PI	PI	PI
21	CP	AQ	AQ	PI	PI	PI	AR
22	AQ	AQ	PI	PI	PI	AR	AR
23	AQ	PI	PI	PI	AR	AR	AR
24	AQ	PI	PI	AR	AR	AR	TA
25	PI	AR	AR	AR	TA	TA	TA
26	PI	AR	AR	TA	TA	TA	GE
27	AR	AR	TA	TA	TA	GE	GE
28	AR	TA	TA	TA	GE	GE	GE
29	AR	TA	TA	GE	GE	GE	CA

AR = Aries, TA = Taurus, GE = Gemini, CA = Cancer, LE = Leo, VI = Virgo, LI = Libra, SC = Scorpio, SA = Sagittarius, CP = Capricorn, AQ = Aquarius, PI = Pisces

MOON SIGNS

Moon in Aries

You have a strong imagination, courage, determination and a desire to do things in your own way and forge your own path through life.

Originality is a key attribute; you are seldom stuck for ideas although your mind is changeable and you could take the time to focus on individual tasks. Often quick-tempered, you take orders from few people and live life at a fast pace. Avoid health problems by taking regular time out for rest and relaxation.

Emotionally, it is important that you talk to those you are closest to and work out your true feelings. Once you discover that people are there to help, there is less necessity for you to do everything yourself.

Moon in Taurus

The Moon in Taurus gives you a courteous and friendly manner, which means you are likely to have many friends.

The good things in life mean a lot to you, as Taurus is an Earth sign that delights in experiences which please the senses. Hence you are probably a lover of good food and drink, which may in turn mean you need to keep an eye on the bathroom scales, especially as looking good is also important to you.

Emotionally you are fairly stable and you stick by your own standards. Taureans do not respond well to change. Intuition also plays an important part in your life.

Moon in Gemini

You have a warm-hearted character, sympathetic and eager to help others. At times reserved, you can also be articulate and chatty: this is part of the paradox of Gemini, which always brings duplicity to the nature. You are interested in current affairs, have a good intellect, and are good company and likely to have many friends. Most of your friends have a high opinion of you and would be ready to defend you should the need arise. However, this is usually unnecessary, as you are quite capable of defending yourself in any verbal confrontation.

Travel is important to your inquisitive mind and you find intellectual stimulus in mixing with people from different cultures. You also gain much from reading, writing and the arts but you do need plenty of rest and relaxation in order to avoid fatigue.

Moon in Cancer

The Moon in Cancer at the time of birth is a fortunate position as Cancer is the Moon's natural home. This means that the qualities of compassion and understanding given by the Moon are especially enhanced in your nature, and you are friendly and sociable and cope well with emotional pressures. You cherish home and family life, and happily do the domestic tasks. Your surroundings are important to you and you hate squalor and filth. You are likely to have a love of music and poetry.

Your basic character, although at times changeable like the Moon itself, depends on symmetry. You aim to make your surroundings comfortable and harmonious, for yourself and those close to you.

Moon in Leo

The best qualities of the Moon and Leo come together to make you warm-hearted, fair, ambitious and self-confident. With good organisational abilities, you invariably rise to a position of responsibility in your chosen career. This is fortunate as you don't enjoy being an 'also-ran' and would rather be an important part of a small organisation than a menial in a large one.

You should be lucky in love, and happy, provided you put in the effort to make a comfortable home for yourself and those close to you. It is likely that you will have a love of pleasure, sport, music and literature. Life brings you many rewards, most of them as a direct result of your own efforts, although you may be luckier than average and ready to make the best of any situation.

Moon in Virgo

You are endowed with good mental abilities and a keen receptive memory, but you are never ostentatious or pretentious. Naturally quite reserved, you still have many friends, especially of the opposite sex. Marital relationships must be discussed carefully and worked at so that they remain harmonious, as personal attachments can be a problem if you do not give them your full attention.

Talented and persevering, you possess artistic qualities and are a good homemaker. Earning your honours through genuine merit, you work long and hard towards your objectives but show little pride in your achievements. Many short journeys will be undertaken in your life.

Moon in Libra

With the Moon in Libra you are naturally popular and make friends easily. People like you, probably more than you realise, you bring fun to a party and are a natural diplomat. For all its good points, Libra is not the most stable of astrological signs and, as a result, your emotions can be a little unstable too. Therefore, although the Moon in Libra is said to be good for love and marriage, your Sun sign and Rising sign will have an important effect on your emotional and loving qualities.

You must remember to relate to others in your decision-making. Co-operation is crucial because Libra represents the 'balance' of life that can only be achieved through harmonious relationships. Conformity is not easy for you because Libra, an Air sign, likes its independence.

Moon in Scorpio

Some people might call you pushy. In fact, all you really want to do is to live life to the full and protect yourself and your family from the pressures of life. Take care to avoid giving the impression of being sarcastic or impulsive and use your energies wisely and constructively.

You have great courage and you invariably achieve your goals by force of personality and sheer effort. You are fond of mystery and are good at predicting the outcome of situations and events. Travel experiences can be beneficial to you.

You may experience problems if you do not take time to examine your motives in a relationship, and also if you allow jealousy, always a feature of Scorpio, to cloud your judgement.

Moon in Sagittarius

The Moon in Sagittarius helps to make you a generous individual with humanitarian qualities and a kind heart. Restlessness may be intrinsic as your mind is seldom still. Perhaps because of this, you have a need for change that could lead you to several major moves during your adult life. You are not afraid to stand your ground when you know your judgement is right, you speak directly and have good intuition.

At work you are quick, efficient and versatile and so you make an ideal employee. You need work to be intellectually demanding and do not enjoy tedious routines.

In relationships, you anger quickly if faced with stupidity or deception, though you are just as quick to forgive and forget. Emotionally, there are times when your heart rules your head.

Moon in Capricorn

The Moon in Capricorn makes you popular and likely to come into the public eye in some way. The watery Moon is not entirely comfortable in the Earth sign of Capricorn and this may lead to some difficulties in the early years of life. An initial lack of creative ability and indecision must be overcome before the true qualities of patience and perseverance inherent in Capricorn can show through.

You have good administrative ability and are a capable worker, and if you are careful you can accumulate wealth. But you must be cautious and take professional advice in partnerships, as you are open to deception. You may be interested in social or welfare work, which suit your organisational skills and sympathy for others.

Moon in Aquarius

The Moon in Aquarius makes you an active and agreeable person with a friendly, easy-going nature. Sympathetic to the needs of others, you flourish in a laid-back atmosphere. You are broad-minded, fair and open to suggestion, although sometimes you have an unconventional quality which others can find hard to understand.

You are interested in the strange and curious, and in old articles and places. You enjoy trips to these places and gain much from them. Political, scientific and educational work interests you and you might choose a career in science or technology.

Money-wise, you make gains through innovation and concentration and Lunar Aquarians often tackle more than one job at a time. In love you are kind and honest.

Moon in Pisces

You have a kind, sympathetic nature, somewhat retiring at times, but you always take account of others' feelings and help when you can.

Personal relationships may be problematic, but as life goes on you can learn from your experiences and develop a better understanding of yourself and the world around you.

You have a fondness for travel, appreciate beauty and harmony and hate disorder and strife. You may be fond of literature and would make a good writer or speaker yourself. You have a creative imagination and may come across as an incurable romantic. You have strong intuition, maybe bordering on a mediumistic quality, which sets you apart from the mass. You may not be rich in cash terms, but your personal gifts are worth more than gold.

GEMINI IN LOVE

Discover how compatible you are with people from the same and other signs of the zodiac. Five stars equals a match made in heaven!

Gemini meets Gemini

Generally speaking, this match can be very successful because although Gemini people can be insecure, they basically feel they are quite 'together' sorts of people. Consequently, they experience a meeting of minds with fellow Twins. This relationship won't work at a distance, and depends on a degree of intimacy to negate the more flighty and showy qualities of the sign. Infidelity could be a potential problem, especially with two Gemini people in the picture, but jealousy doesn't usually prevail. Star rating: ****

Gemini meets Cancer

This is often a very good match. Cancer is a very caring sign and quite adaptable. Geminis are untidy, have butterfly minds and are usually full of a thousand different schemes which Cancerians take in their stride and even relish. They can often be the 'wind beneath the wings' of their Gemini partners. In return, Gemini can eradicate some of the Cancerian emotional insecurity and is more likely to be faithful in thought, word and deed to Cancer than to almost any other sign. Star rating: ****

Gemini meets Leo

There can be problems here, but Gemini is adaptable enough to overcome many of them. Leo is a go-getter and might sometimes rail against Gemini's flighty tendencies, while Gemini's mental disorganisation can undermine Leo's practicality. However, Leo is cheerful and enjoys Gemini's jokey, flippant qualities. At times of personal intimacy, the two signs should be compatible. Leo and Gemini share very high ideals, but Leo will stick at them for longer. Patience is needed on both sides for the relationship to develop. Star rating: ***

Gemini meets Virgo

The fact that both these signs are ruled by the planet Mercury might at first seem good but, unfortunately, Mercury works very differently in each of them. Gemini is untidy, flighty, quick, changeable and easily bored, while Virgo is fastidious, steady and constant. If Virgo is willing to accept some anarchy, all can be well, but this not usually the case. Virgoans are deep thinkers and may find Gemini a little superficial. This pair can be compatible intellectually, though even this side isn't without its problems. Star rating: ***

Gemini meets Libra

One of the best possible zodiac combinations. Libra and Gemini are both Air signs, which leads to a meeting of minds. Both signs simply love to have a good time, although Libra is the tidiest and less forgetful. Gemini's capricious nature won't bother Libra, who acts as a stabilising influence. Life should generally run smoothly, and any rows are likely to be short and sharp. Both parties genuinely like each other, which is of paramount importance in a relationship and, ultimately, there isn't a better reason for being or staying together. Star rating: *****

Gemini meets Scorpio

There could be problems here. Scorpio is one of the deepest and least understood of all the zodiac signs, which at first seems like a challenge to intellectual Gemini, who thinks it can solve anything. But the deeper the Gemini digs, the further down Scorpio goes. Meanwhile, Scorpio may be finding Gemini thoughtless, shallow and even downright annoying. Gemini is often afraid of Scorpio's strength, and the sting in its tail, both of which the perceptive Twins can instinctively recognise. Anything is possible, but the outlook for this match is less than promising. Star rating: **

Gemini meets Sagittarius

A paradoxical relationship this. On paper, the two signs have much in common, but unfortunately, they are often so alike that life turns into a fiercely fought competition. Both signs love change and diversity and both want to be the life and soul of the party. But in life there must always be a leader and a follower, and neither of this pair wants to be second. Both also share a tendency towards infidelity, which may develop into a problem as time passes. This could be an interesting match, but not necessarily successful. Star rating: **

Gemini meets Capricorn

Gemini has a natural fondness for Capricorn, which at first may be mutual. However, Capricorn is very organised, practical and persevering, and always achieves its goals in the end. Gemini starts out like this, but then changes direction on the way, using a more instinctive and evolutionary approach than the Goat that may interfere with the progress of mutual objectives. To compensate, Gemini helps Capricorn to avoid taking itself too seriously, while Capricorn brings a degree of stability into Gemini's world. When this pairing does work, though, it will be spectacular! Star rating: ***

Gemini meets Aquarius

Aquarius is commonly mistaken for a Water sign, but in fact it's ruled by the Air element, and this is the key to its compatibility with Gemini. Both signs mix freely socially, and each has an insatiable curiosity. There is plenty of action, lots of love but very little rest, and so great potential for success if they don't wear each other out! Aquarius revels in its own eccentricity, and encourages Gemini to emulate this. Theirs will be an unconventional household, but almost everyone warms to this crazy and unpredictable couple. Star rating: *****

Gemini meets Pisces

Gemini likes to think of itself as intuitive and intellectual, and indeed sometimes it is, but it will never understand Pisces' dark depths. Another stumbling block is that both Gemini and Pisces are 'split' signs – the Twins and the two Fishes – which means that both are capable of dual personalities. There won't be any shortage of affection, but the real question has to be how much these people ultimately feel they have in common. Pisces is extremely kind, and so is Gemini most of the time. But Pisces does altogether too much soul-searching for Gemini, who might eventually become bored. Star rating: ***

Gemini meets Aries

Don't expect peace and harmony with this combination, although what comes along instead might make up for any disagreements. Gemini has a very fertile imagination, while Aries has the tenacity to make reality from fantasy. Combined, they have a sizzling relationship. There are times when it seems as though both parties will explode with indignation and something has to give. But even if there are clashes, making them up will always be most enjoyable! Mutual financial success is very likely in this match. Star rating: ****

Gemini meets Taurus

Gemini people can really infuriate the generally steady Taurean nature as they are so untidy, which is a complete reversal of the Taurean ethos. At first this won't matter; Mr or Miss Gemini is enchanting, entertaining and very different. But time will tell, and that's why this potential relationship only has two stars. There is some hope, however, because Taurus can curb some of the excesses of the Twins, whilst Gemini is more than capable of preventing the Bull from taking itself too seriously. Star rating: **

31

VENUS:
THE PLANET OF LOVE

If you look up at the sky around sunset or sunrise you will often see Venus in close attendance to the Sun. It is arguably one of the most beautiful sights of all and there is little wonder that historically it became associated with the goddess of love. But although Venus does play an important part in the way you view love and in the way others see you romantically, this is only one of the spheres of influence that it enjoys in your overall character.

Venus has a part to play in the more cultured side of your life and has much to do with your appreciation of art, literature, music and general creativity. Even the way you look is responsive to the part of the zodiac that Venus occupied at the start of your life, though this fact is also down to your Sun sign and Ascending sign. If, at the time you were born, Venus occupied one of the more gregarious zodiac signs, you will be more likely to wear your heart on your sleeve, as well as to be more attracted to entertainment, social gatherings and good company. If on the other hand Venus occupied a quiet zodiac sign at the time of your birth, you would tend to be more retiring and less willing to shine in public situations.

It's good to know what part the planet Venus plays in your life for it can have a great bearing on the way you appear to the rest of the world and since we all have to mix with others, you can learn to make the very best of what Venus has to offer you.

One of the great complications in the past has always been trying to establish exactly what zodiac position Venus enjoyed when you were born because the planet is notoriously difficult to track. However, I have solved that problem by creating a table that is exclusive to your Sun sign, which you will find on the following page.

Establishing your Venus sign could not be easier. Just look up the year of your birth on the page opposite and you will see a sign of the zodiac. This was the sign that Venus occupied in the period covered by your sign in that year. If Venus occupied more than one sign during the period, this is indicated by the date on which the sign changed, and the name of the new sign. For instance, if you were born in 1950, Venus was in Gemini until the 8th June, after which time it was in Cancer. If you were born before 8th June your Venus sign is Gemini, if you were born on or after 8th June, your Venus sign is Cancer. Once you have established the position of Venus at the time of your birth, you can then look in the pages which follow to see how this has a bearing on your life as a whole.

1911 CANCER / 8.6 LEO
1912 TAURUS / 1.6 GEMINI
1913 ARIES / 31.4 TAURUS
1914 GEMINI / 26.5 CANCER
1915 ARIES / 22.5 TAURUS /
    16.6 GEMINI
1916 CANCER
1917 GEMINI / 10.6 CANCER
1918 ARIES / 3.6 TAURUS
1919 CANCER / 8.6 LEO
1920 TAURUS / 3.6 GEMINI
1921 ARIES / 3.6 TAURUS
1922 GEMINI / 26.5 CANCER /
    21.6 LEO
1923 TAURUS / 15.6 GEMINI
1924 CANCER
1925 GEMINI / 9.6 CANCER
1926 ARIES / 2.6 TAURUS
1927 CANCER / 8.6 LEO
1928 TAURUS / 30.5 GEMINI
1929 ARIES / 4.6 TAURUS
1930 GEMINI / 22.5 CANCER /
    21.6 LEO
1931 TAURUS / 15.6 GEMINI
1932 CANCER
1933 GEMINI / 9.6 CANCER
1934 ARIES / 2.6 TAURUS
1935 CANCER / 8.6 LEO
1936 TAURUS / 30.5 GEMINI
1937 ARIES / 4.6 TAURUS
1938 GEMINI / 25.5 CANCER /
    20.6 LEO
1939 TAURUS / 14.6 GEMINI
1940 CANCER
1941 CANCER / 7.6 LEO
1942 GEMINI / 8.6 CANCER
1943 ARIES / 1.6 TAURUS
1944 CANCER / 7.6 LEO
1945 TAURUS / 29.5 GEMINI
1946 ARIES / 5.6 TAURUS
1947 GEMINI / 24.5 CANCER /
    19.6 LEO
1948 TAURUS / 14.6 GEMINI
1949 CANCER
1950 GEMINI / 8.6 CANCER
1951 ARIES / 1.6 TAURUS
1952 TAURUS / 29.5 GEMINI
1953 ARIES / 5.6 TAURUS
1954 GEMINI / 24.5 CANCER /
    19.6 LEO
1955 TAURUS / 13.6 GEMINI
1956 CANCER
1957 GEMINI / 7.6 CANCER
1958 ARIES / 31.5 TAURUS
1959 CANCER / 7.6 LEO
1960 TAURUS / 28.5 GEMINI
1961 ARIES / 6.6 TAURUS

1962 GEMINI / 24.5 CANCER /
    18.6 LEO
1963 TAURUS / 13.6 GEMINI
1964 CANCER / 17.6 GEMINI
1965 GEMINI / 7.6 CANCER
1966 ARIES / 31.5 TAURUS
1967 CANCER / 7.6 LEO
1968 TAURUS / 28.5 GEMINI
1969 ARIES / 6.6 TAURUS
1970 GEMINI / 23.5 CANCER /
    18.5 LEO
1971 TAURUS / 12.6 GEMINI
1972 CANCER / 12.6 GEMINI
1973 GEMINI / 6.6 CANCER
1974 ARIES / 30.5 TAURUS
1975 CANCER / 7.6 LEO
1976 TAURUS / 27.5 GEMINI
1977 ARIES / 7.6 TAURUS
1978 GEMINI / 23.5 CANCER /
    17.5 LEO
1979 TAURUS / 12.6 GEMINI
1980 CANCER / 6.6 GEMINI
1981 GEMINI / 6.6 CANCER
1982 ARIES / 30.5 TAURUS
1983 CANCER / 6.6 LEO
1984 TAURUS / 27.5 GEMINI /
    21.6 CANCER
1985 ARIES / 7.6 TAURUS
1986 GEMINI / 22.5 CANCER /
    17.5 LEO
1987 TAURUS / 11.6 GEMINI
1988 CANCER / 27.5 GEMINI
1989 GEMINI / 5.6 CANCER
1990 ARIES / 29.5 TAURUS
1991 CANCER / 6.6 LEO
1992 TAURUS / 26.5 GEMINI /
    20.6 CANCER
1993 ARIES / 7.6 TAURUS
1994 CANCER / 16.6 LEO
1995 TAURUS / 11.6 GEMINI
1996 CANCER / 27.5 GEMINI
1997 GEMINI / 4.6 CANCER
1998 ARIES / 29.5 TAURUS
1999 CANCER / 6.6 LEO
2000 TAURUS / 25.5 GEMINI /
    19.6 CANCER
2001 ARIES / 7.6 TAURUS
2002 CANCER / 15.6 LEO
2003 TAURUS / 11.6 GEMINI
2004 CANCER / 27.5 GEMINI
2005 GEMINI / 2.6 CANCER
2006 ARIES / 29.6 TAURUS
2007 CANCER / 6.6 LEO
2008 TAURUS / 25.5 GEMINI /
    19.6 CANCER
2009 ARIES / 7.6 TAURUS

VENUS THROUGH THE ZODIAC SIGNS

Venus in Aries

Amongst other things, the position of Venus in Aries indicates a fondness for travel, music and all creative pursuits. Your nature tends to be affectionate and you would try not to create confusion or difficulty for others if it could be avoided. Many people with this planetary position have a great love of the theatre, and mental stimulation is of the greatest importance. Early romantic attachments are common with Venus in Aries, so it is very important to establish a genuine sense of romantic continuity. Early marriage is not recommended, especially if it is based on sympathy. You may give your heart a little too readily on occasions.

Venus in Taurus

You are capable of very deep feelings and your emotions tend to last for a very long time. This makes you a trusting partner and lover, whose constancy is second to none. In life you are precise and careful and always try to do things the right way. Although this means an ordered life, which you are comfortable with, it can also lead you to be rather too fussy for your own good. Despite your pleasant nature, you are very fixed in your opinions and quite able to speak your mind. Others are attracted to you and historical astrologers always quoted this position of Venus as being very fortunate in terms of marriage. However, if you find yourself involved in a failed relationship, it could take you a long time to trust again.

Venus in Gemini

As with all associations related to Gemini, you tend to be quite versatile, anxious for change and intelligent in your dealings with the world at large. You may gain money from more than one source but you are equally good at spending it. There is an inference here that you are a good communicator, via either the written or the spoken word, and you love to be in the company of interesting people. Always on the look-out for culture, you may also be very fond of music, and love to indulge the curious and cultured side of your nature. In romance you tend to have more than one relationship and could find yourself associated with someone who has previously been a friend or even a distant relative.

Venus in Cancer

You often stay close to home because you are very fond of family and enjoy many of your most treasured moments when you are with those you love. Being naturally sympathetic, you will always do anything you can to support those around you, even people you hardly know at all. This charitable side of your nature is your most noticeable trait and is one of the reasons why others are naturally so fond of you. Being receptive and in some cases even psychic, you can see through to the soul of most of those with whom you come into contact. You may not commence too many romantic attachments but when you do give your heart, it tends to be unconditionally.

Venus in Leo

It must become quickly obvious to almost anyone you meet that you are kind, sympathetic and yet determined enough to stand up for anyone or anything that is truly important to you. Bright and sunny, you warm the world with your natural enthusiasm and would rarely do anything to hurt those around you, or at least not intentionally. In romance you are ardent and sincere, though some may find your style just a little overpowering. Gains come through your contacts with other people and this could be especially true with regard to romance, for love and money often come hand in hand for those who were born with Venus in Leo. People claim to understand you, though you are more complex than you seem.

Venus in Virgo

Your nature could well be fairly quiet no matter what your Sun sign might be, though this fact often manifests itself as an inner peace and would not prevent you from being basically sociable. Some delays and even the odd disappointment in love cannot be ruled out with this planetary position, though it's a fact that you will usually find the happiness you look for in the end. Catapulting yourself into romantic entanglements that you know to be rather ill-advised is not sensible, and it would be better to wait before you committed yourself exclusively to any one person. It is the essence of your nature to serve the world at large and through doing so it is possible that you will attract money at some stage in your life.

Venus in Libra

Venus is very comfortable in Libra and bestows upon those people who have this planetary position a particular sort of kindness that is easy to recognise. This is a very good position for all sorts of friendships and also for romantic attachments that usually bring much joy into your life. Few individuals with Venus in Libra would avoid marriage and since you are capable of great depths of love, it is likely that you will find a contented personal life. You like to mix with people of integrity and intelligence but don't take kindly to scruffy surroundings or work that means getting your hands too dirty. Careful speculation, good business dealings and money through marriage all seem fairly likely.

Venus in Scorpio

You are quite open and tend to spend money quite freely, even on those occasions when you don't have very much. Although your intentions are always good, there are times when you get yourself in to the odd scrape and this can be particularly true when it comes to romance, which you may come to late or from a rather unexpected direction. Certainly you have the power to be happy and to make others contented on the way, but you find the odd stumbling block on your journey through life and it could seem that you have to work harder than those around you. As a result of this, you gain a much deeper understanding of the true value of personal happiness than many people ever do, and are likely to achieve true contentment in the end.

Venus in Sagittarius

You are lighthearted, cheerful and always able to see the funny side of any situation. These facts enhance your popularity, which is especially high with members of the opposite sex. You should never have to look too far to find romantic interest in your life, though it is just possible that you might be too willing to commit yourself before you are certain that the person in question is right for you. Part of the problem here extends to other areas of life too. The fact is that you like variety in everything and so can tire of situations that fail to offer it. All the same, if you choose wisely and learn to understand your restless side, then great happiness can be yours.

Venus in Capricorn

The most notable trait that comes from Venus in this position is that it makes you trustworthy and able to take on all sorts of responsibilities in life. People are instinctively fond of you and love you all the more because you are always ready to help those who are in any form of need. Social and business popularity can be yours and there is a magnetic quality to your nature that is particularly attractive in a romantic sense. Anyone who wants a partner for a lover, a spouse and a good friend too would almost certainly look in your direction. Constancy is the hallmark of your nature and unfaithfulness would go right against the grain. You might sometimes be a little too trusting.

Venus in Aquarius

This location of Venus offers a fondness for travel and a desire to try out something new at every possible opportunity. You are extremely easy to get along with and tend to have many friends from varied backgrounds, classes and inclinations. You like to live a distinct sort of life and gain a great deal from moving about, both in a career sense and with regard to your home. It is not out of the question that you could form a romantic attachment to someone who comes from far away or be attracted to a person of a distinctly artistic and original nature. What you cannot stand is jealousy, for you have friends of both sexes and would want to keep things that way.

Venus in Pisces

The first thing people tend to notice about you is your wonderful, warm smile. Being very charitable by nature you will do anything to help others, even if you don't know them well. Much of your life may be spent sorting out situations for other people, but it is very important to feel that you are living for yourself too. In the main, you remain cheerful, and tend to be quite attractive to members of the opposite sex. Where romantic attachments are concerned, you could be drawn to people who are significantly older or younger than yourself or to someone with a unique career or point of view. It might be best for you to avoid marrying whilst you are still very young.

THE ASTRAL DIARY
HOW THE DIAGRAMS WORK

Through the picture diagrams in the Astral Diary I want to help you to plot your year. With them you can see where the positive and negative aspects will be found in each month. To make the most of them, all you have to do is remember where and when!

Let me show you how they work ...

THE MONTH AT A GLANCE

Just as there are twelve separate zodiac signs, so astrologers believe that each sign has twelve separate aspects to life. Each of the twelve segments relates to a different personal aspect. I list them all every month so that their meanings are always clear.

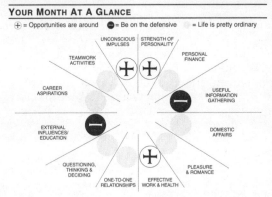

YOUR MONTH AT A GLANCE

⊕ = Opportunities are around   ⊖ = Be on the defensive   = Life is pretty ordinary

UNCONSCIOUS IMPULSES

STRENGTH OF PERSONALITY

TEAMWORK ACTIVITIES

PERSONAL FINANCE

CAREER ASPIRATIONS

USEFUL INFORMATION GATHERING

EXTERNAL INFLUENCES/ EDUCATION

DOMESTIC AFFAIRS

QUESTIONING, THINKING & DECIDING

PLEASURE & ROMANCE

ONE-TO-ONE RELATIONSHIPS

EFFECTIVE WORK & HEALTH

I have designed this chart to show you how and when these twelve different aspects are being influenced throughout the year. When there is a shaded circle, nothing out of the ordinary is to be expected. However, when a circle turns white with a plus sign, the influence is positive. Where the circle is black with a minus sign, it is a negative.

YOUR ENERGY RHYTHM CHART

On the opposite page is a picture diagram in which I am linking your zodiac group to the rhythm of the Moon. In doing this I have calculated when you will be gaining strength from its influence and equally when you may be weakened by it.

If you think of yourself as being like the tides of the ocean then you may understand how your own energies must also rise and fall. And if you understand how it works and when it is working, then you can better organise your activities to achieve more and get things done more easily.

YOUR ENERGY RHYTHM CHART

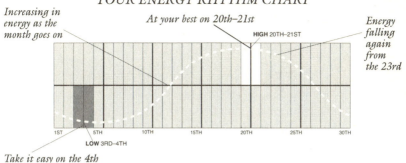

Increasing in energy as the month goes on

At your best on 20th–21st

HIGH 20TH–21ST

Energy falling again from the 23rd

1ST   5TH   10TH   15TH   20TH   25TH   30TH

LOW 3RD–4TH

Take it easy on the 4th

MOVING PICTURE SCREEN
Love, money, career and vitality measured every week

The diagram at the end of each week is designed to be informative and fun. The arrows move up and down the scale to give you an idea of the strength of your opportunities in each area. If LOVE stands at plus 4, then get out and put yourself about because things are going your way in romance! The further down the arrow goes, the weaker the opportunities. Do note that the diagram is an overall view of your astrological aspects and therefore reflects a trend which may not concur with every day in that cycle.

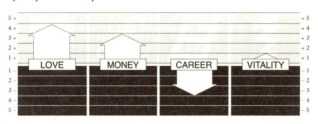

AND FINALLY:

am . . . .

pm . . . .

The two lines that are left blank in each daily entry of the Astral Diary are for your own personal use. You may find them ideal for keeping a check on birthdays or appointments, though it could be an idea to make notes from the astrological trends and diagrams a few weeks in advance. Some of the lines are marked with a key, which indicates the working of astrological cycles in your life. Look out for them each week as they are the best days to take action or make decisions. The daily text tells you which area of your life to focus on.

☿ = Mercury is retrograde on that day.

GEMINI: YOUR YEAR IN BRIEF

It might seem at the start of this year that you are not making the progress you would wish but this is nothing more than a temporary matter and within a few days everything should be on course again. January and February should find you willing to take on new projects, happy to co-operate with others and quite determined to make headway. Some personal matters could be complicated and a little extra thought will be necessary.

The months of March and April could bring a few complications on the personal front but nothing that will be too difficult. As is often the case for Gemini worries soon vaporise like the morning mist and you will be anxious during most months to make better use of your skills and gifts. The response from family members at this time should be good and you will revel in the love and support they offer.

The late spring will be quite delightful for most sons and daughters of Gemini. You will be at your most charming and well able to get others to do your bidding, simply by asking. Money matters should be easier to deal with and both May and June bring you closer to achieving longed-for objectives, especially in the sphere of work and new interests. You could be quite competitive at this time and may be taking up new activities that test you more than usual.

With July and August more care is necessary over details. Most aspects of life ought to be going your way but there can be complications if you leave things to chance. It would be better to repeat tasks than to risk losing out and you can also respond to the assistance offered by colleagues and friends. This is a time for getting out and about, enjoying yourself in the best company and making a positive impression.

The months of September and October see you taking trips and possibly considering a late holiday. Your general level of good luck is likely to be better and you will be steaming ahead towards any professional objectives. Love looks good at this time and you should be in the market for an interesting new start on the home front. Maybe you are re-organising, redecorating or even moving house. Anything you plan around now is likely to turn out very much as you intend.

With the end of the year comes an extra series of incentives and a push towards finishing those tasks that you set yourself way back in January. It looks as though both November and December are going to be very busy for most Gemini people and there won't be as much time as you would wish for Christmas preparations. When it comes to enjoyment you finish the year with a definite flourish and that is what counts.

January
2009

YOUR MONTH AT A GLANCE

⊕ = Opportunities are around   ⊖ = Be on the defensive   = Life is pretty ordinary

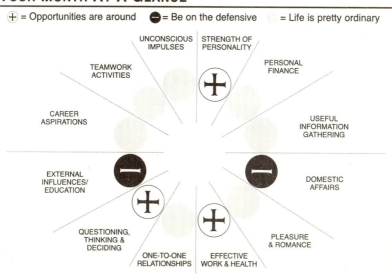

JANUARY HIGHS AND LOWS

Here I show you how the rhythms of the Moon will affect you this month. Like the tide, your energies and abilities will rise and fall with its pattern. When it is above the centre line, go for it, when it is below, you should be resting.

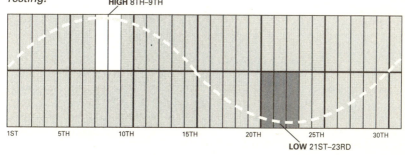

29 MONDAY

Moon Age Day 2   Moon Sign Capricorn

am . . . .

pm . . . .
Today responds best if you spend time communicating with people in the outside world – which is of course the way you most love things to be. This is the best period of the month for any sort of excursion and you should also be able to get your mind working on about seventy-five different levels at the same time.

30 TUESDAY

Moon Age Day 3   Moon Sign Aquarius

am . . . .

pm . . . .
If you are at work this week you might discover that colleagues and superiors are relying on you quite heavily. For those of you who are still on holiday, there are likely to be new situations coming along and the chance to make a really good impression on someone whose opinion is very important to you.

31 WEDNESDAY

Moon Age Day 4   Moon Sign Aquarius

am . . . .

pm . . . .
Even if there is now a conflict between what you want and what pleases those with whom you live, you can make slight alterations that will see the day passing happily. Most important of all are the social possibilities because by tonight you can afford to party your socks off!

1 THURSDAY

Moon Age Day 5   Moon Sign Aquarius

am . . . .

pm . . . .
Start the New Year as you mean to go on by showing your drive and determination. There are plenty of people around now who can be persuaded to listen to what you have to say. Any obstacles that probably seemed particularly difficult to deal with only a week or two ago can now be dealt with in a few moments.

2 FRIDAY
Moon Age Day 6   Moon Sign Pisces

am . . . .

pm . . . .
Being right seems very important at present, so it's worth getting people
to listen to your point of view. That's fine just as long as you really do
know what you are talking about. If you end up having to admit you
were wrong you could lose face, and to a Gemini that can be quite a
serious matter. 'Think first' is the adage.

3 SATURDAY
Moon Age Day 7   Moon Sign Pisces

am . . . .

pm . . . .
A day to get on side with people who are going places, and then you can
ride their vehicle to your own success. You always are a good co-operator
but it is especially important at the moment to throw in your lot with
others. You can best avoid family arguments by removing yourself from
the possibility of them and mixing more with friends.

4 SUNDAY
Moon Age Day 8   Moon Sign Aries

am . . . .

pm . . . .
Some of the things that happen today might not seem to be in your best
interest, but in the fullness of time you can make sure that life is going
your way in a general sense. There are some minor frustrations about but
you will have to take these in your stride. Why not get on with jobs that
need to be out of the way before a new week begins?

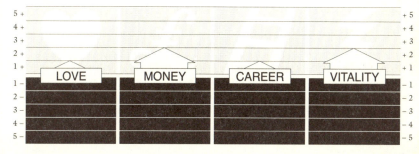

5 MONDAY
Moon Age Day 9   Moon Sign Aries

am . . . .

pm . . . .
You can find plenty to keep you occupied today, and have what it takes to be on top form, especially in a social sense. With people gathering around you all the time this would be a good period to ask for something you really want. Communication counts for a great deal now.

6 TUESDAY
Moon Age Day 10   Moon Sign Taurus

am . . . .

pm . . . .
Things might get a little quieter for the next couple of days because ahead of the Moon entering Gemini it passes through your solar twelfth house. This supports a slightly more reflective phase when you are inclined to seek your own company. All the same there is still plenty happening around you that could be seen as distinctly positive.

7 WEDNESDAY
Moon Age Day 11   Moon Sign Taurus

am . . . .

pm . . . .
Reputations could well be at stake today, especially if someone is saying something about you that is definitely not true. By all means defend yourself, though there is a chance that if you do so with too much apparent conviction you might make things worse. Don't be afraid to leave well enough alone for the moment.

8 THURSDAY
Moon Age Day 12   Moon Sign Gemini

am . . . .

pm . . . .
Now the Moon enters your own zodiac sign of Gemini, bringing with it that part of the month that is known as the lunar high. You have scope to be on top form and should be up for any sort of excitement. Be prepared to use today to get those you really care about on your side.

9 FRIDAY

Moon Age Day 13   Moon Sign Gemini

am . . . .

pm . . . .

Things should still be looking good as the weekend approaches. Finish the working week with a definite flourish and do what you can to get ahead in the business stakes. If you keep Lady Luck on your side you can afford to take the odd chance. Keep your gambling to a minimum though because good luck only stretches so far.

10 SATURDAY

Moon Age Day 14   Moon Sign Cancer

am . . . .

pm . . . .

Your charming personal manner can help you to maintain your popularity and you have what it takes to impress important people. Socially speaking you should be on form and mixing with as many different sorts of individuals as turns out to be possible.

11 SUNDAY

Moon Age Day 15   Moon Sign Cancer

am . . . .

pm . . . .

With a somewhat quieter day on offer, it's worth catching up on jobs at home, though you may not be glad of your own company all day long. Later on you might decide to be out there amongst your friends, proving that you are the liveliest individual of them all. You won't have to try very hard, since everyone knows!

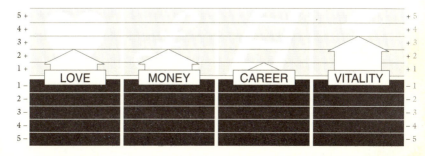

12 MONDAY ☿ *Moon Age Day 16   Moon Sign Leo*

am . . . .

pm . . . .
You can afford to quicken the pace of your life again as the normal responsibilities of the working week start to catch up with you. Not that this is any sort of problem. You know what you want from life at present and will have a very good idea about how you can get it. Make the most of new contacts this week.

13 TUESDAY ☿ *Moon Age Day 17   Moon Sign Leo*

am . . . .

pm . . . .
The more you learn about things, the greater is your capacity to put what you know to the test. Capitalise on startling insights and maybe even one or two ridiculous coincidences. A greater than usual sense of responsibility seems to be heading your way, assisting you to be particularly protective of family members and old friends.

14 WEDNESDAY ☿ *Moon Age Day 18   Moon Sign Virgo*

am . . . .

pm . . . .
There isn't any doubt about your present capacity for work. You can do whatever is demanded of you in an instant and the impossible takes only a while longer. If you are generally contented with your lot, you can push ahead progressively in the sure and certain knowledge that everything you do contributes to your eventual success.

15 THURSDAY ☿ *Moon Age Day 19   Moon Sign Virgo*

am . . . .

pm . . . .
There may be a lot of promises around at the moment and although many of them are gratifying, in the end you would be wise to be very careful. Get-rich-quick schemes should probably be avoided altogether for the moment, in favour of slow and steady progress. This isn't quite so appealing, but is a darn sight safer in the long run.

16 FRIDAY ☿ *Moon Age Day 20 Moon Sign Libra*

am . . . .

pm . . . .
As you make your way up the ladder of achievement, you might catch sight of one or two individuals who are definitely coming in the opposite direction. Show some care and concern because it is your true humanity that often sets you apart. Gemini can be very charity-minded in all sorts of ways at the moment.

17 SATURDAY ☿ *Moon Age Day 21 Moon Sign Libra*

am . . . .

pm . . . .
Gemini is not generally known for its patience. You want everything available and you want it right now. This may not be possible for today at least, so be prepared to set your sights somewhat lower than might normally be the case. Confidential conversations are best kept that way.

18 SUNDAY ☿ *Moon Age Day 22 Moon Sign Libra*

am . . . .

pm . . . .
Rules and regulations have potential to get on your nerves, and especially on a Sunday. Why not fight shy of them today and do something different? Get out of the house with your partner or friends and just have a good time. No matter what you choose to do, you have scope to show your panache.

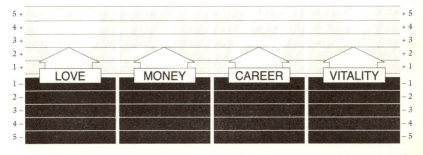

19 MONDAY ☿ *Moon Age Day 23 Moon Sign Scorpio*

am . . . .

pm . . . .
Although it's only January you could already be feeling the need for a general spring-clean. It isn't so much your possessions that need sorting out as your inner mind. If you are hanging onto thoughts and possibilities that no longer have any real relevance to your life, you need to get things sorted out. A chat with a good friend might help.

20 TUESDAY ☿ *Moon Age Day 24 Moon Sign Scorpio*

am . . . .

pm . . . .
The greatest fulfilment of all at this time lies in personal freedom and the sense that you are doing what appeals to you the most. It's worth avoiding family arguments and playing the honest broker on all occasions. As usual you probably have a thousand different things that you want to do and a very limited amount of time to fit it all in.

21 WEDNESDAY ☿ *Moon Age Day 25 Moon Sign Sagittarius*

am . . . .

pm . . . .
A day to box clever and allow someone else to take some of the strain. Now the Moon has moved into your opposite zodiac sign, bringing that time of the month that is known as the lunar low. Attitude is the most important factor, together with being willing to slow down and take stock. Real activity is best saved until later this week.

22 THURSDAY ☿ *Moon Age Day 26 Moon Sign Sagittarius*

am . . . .

pm . . . .
Social relationships are favoured, even if there is a part of you that really wants to curl up in a corner and be alone. This causes something of a dichotomy, one that often prevails in the life of Gemini. Mix and match is the best way forward. You can move forward as you wish, just as long as you are sensible in the way you go about it.

23 FRIDAY
☿ *Moon Age Day 27   Moon Sign Sagittarius*

am . . . .

pm . . . .
For the third day in a row, drive and enthusiasm may be hard to summon. Fortunately these trends will be well out of the way before the weekend arrives, leaving you with greater energy and a significant opportunity to get ahead. For the moment you can afford to watch and wait – even drifting with the tide.

24 SATURDAY
☿ *Moon Age Day 28   Moon Sign Capricorn*

am . . . .

pm . . . .
New responsibilities are in view, but that needn't trouble you in the slightest. The fact is that you can now be fully back on form and quite willing to take on whatever life wants to throw at you. With new incentives on offer all the time, today could seem like a time when you have just woken from a deep sleep. It's upward and onward!

25 SUNDAY
☿ *Moon Age Day 29   Moon Sign Capricorn*

am . . . .

pm . . . .
Sort out your finances today if it proves to be possible – even if this means getting to grips with other family members and their spending habits. You can be very diplomatic at present and shouldn't have any difficulty at all explaining your point of view. Your strength lies in sorting out other people's messes too.

5 +				+ 5
4 +				+ 4
3 +				+ 3
2 +				+ 2
1 +				+ 1
1 -	LOVE	MONEY	CAREER	VITALITY	- 1
2 -				- 2
3 -				- 3
4 -				- 4
5 -				- 5

26 MONDAY ☿ *Moon Age Day 0   Moon Sign Aquarius*

am . . . .

pm . . . .
Although a new working week begins today, the accent is definitely on the social side of your life. This encourages you either to push your personality into your work, or to do less in a practical sense in favour of pleasing yourself and mixing more freely. Someone special may be on your mind for most of today.

27 TUESDAY ☿ *Moon Age Day 1   Moon Sign Aquarius*

am . . . .

pm . . . .
It might be best to assume a lower profile in some areas of life, so that you can spend more time and effort in other directions. There are financial gains to be made at almost every turn, but you need to be quick and astute if you are going to make the very best out of what surrounds you. Confidence is definitely well accented.

28 WEDNESDAY ☿ *Moon Age Day 2   Moon Sign Aquarius*

am . . . .

pm . . . .
Trends suggest that it isn't the mainstream of life that appeals to you greatly today but rather its undercurrents. Be prepared to find out how everything works and to discover what is really going on. With your detective head on you can get to the bottom of something that has been on your mind for a very long time now.

29 THURSDAY ☿ *Moon Age Day 3   Moon Sign Pisces*

am . . . .

pm . . . .
In some situations it seems as though you have dropped off the end of the page because you really don't seem to know what is happening. This may well be because of the disorganisation of others rather than your own attitudes or aptitudes. Ask for a better explanation and if that doesn't work, ask again.

30 FRIDAY ☿ *Moon Age Day 4* *Moon Sign Pisces*

am . . . .

pm . . . .
You may not feel exactly up for a challenge just now and will be happier than usual to let things ride. This is a very temporary factor, brought about by the position of the Moon. All too soon you can put yourself back in the driving seat and get involved. Trends also assist you to respond to the demands of friends.

31 SATURDAY ☿ *Moon Age Day 5* *Moon Sign Aries*

am . . . .

pm . . . .
Standard responses probably won't be enough when it comes to family members. They want to know exactly what you have on your mind and won't be fudged. Maybe it's time to come clean and to tell the truth. The only problem is that there are times when Gemini wouldn't know the real truth if it bit them on the bottom. Confusion is possible.

1 SUNDAY *Moon Age Day 6* *Moon Sign Aries*

am . . . .

pm . . . .
The start of a new month brings incentives galore, even if you don't recognise the fact at first. There ought to be time today to please yourself and to do whatever takes your personal fancy. If this is not the case, perhaps you are doing too much for someone else. Encouraging them to stand on their own feet would be no bad thing.

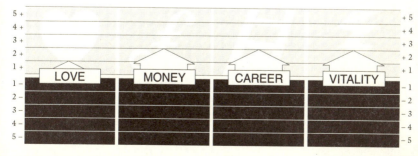

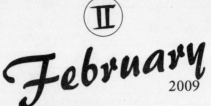

February 2009

YOUR MONTH AT A GLANCE

⊕ = Opportunities are around   ⊖ = Be on the defensive   ◯ = Life is pretty ordinary

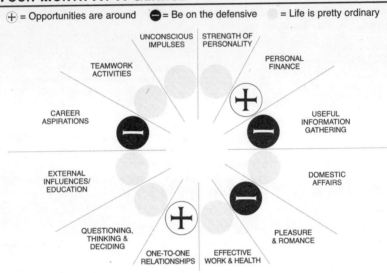

FEBRUARY HIGHS AND LOWS

Here I show you how the rhythms of the Moon will affect you this month. Like the tide, your energies and abilities will rise and fall with its pattern. When it is above the centre line, go for it, when it is below, you should be resting.

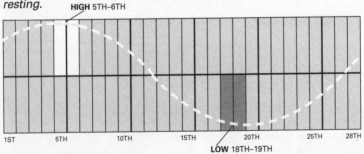

HIGH 5TH–6TH

LOW 18TH–19TH

2 MONDAY
Moon Age Day 7   Moon Sign Taurus

am . . . .

pm . . . .
Three fairly quiet and nondescript days lie before you – at least they will unless you take control. The Moon is in your solar twelfth house and that isn't conducive to making you energetic. In the end that doesn't matter, because there are ways and means of getting ahead without putting in the effort yourself.

3 TUESDAY
Moon Age Day 8   Moon Sign Taurus

am . . . .

pm . . . .
Things generally should be set fair and you needn't view either today or the future with too much in the way of pessimism. All the same life could lack some zing, and that can only be engendered by your own attitude. If there is something you want, by all means don't take no for an answer, but on the other hand don't sulk.

4 WEDNESDAY
Moon Age Day 9   Moon Sign Taurus

am . . . .

pm . . . .
You can afford to rely heavily on what colleagues and friends have to say to you. There could be information about now that can be a real help later but if you don't keep your ears open you might miss it. The planetary focus is also on current affairs, and on keeping busy.

5 THURSDAY
Moon Age Day 10   Moon Sign Gemini

am . . . .

pm . . . .
Everything you have been watching and hearing over the last two or three days can now be put to good use. You have what it takes to get fully back on form and to get involved with life at every level. Just remember that although this is the lunar high you are not a one-person working machine. Why not take rest later in the day?

6 FRIDAY   *Moon Age Day 11   Moon Sign Gemini*

am . . . .

pm . . . .
What really sets today apart is the level to which you become involved with others. Both at work and later in a social sense you have scope to be the life and soul of any party – some of which you might be organising in any case. Rely on your instincts now in order to get ahead. That intuition of yours is highlighted, and shouldn't let you down.

7 SATURDAY   *Moon Age Day 12   Moon Sign Cancer*

am . . . .

pm . . . .
Gemini is much more courageous than it thinks and you have a chance to prove the fact today by stepping in to defend someone you consider is being wronged. You can use this outspoken attitude to get yourself noticed and to show others you are an honourable and truthful friend. Try to get your own way today without making any enemies.

8 SUNDAY   *Moon Age Day 13   Moon Sign Cancer*

am . . . .

pm . . . .
If the weekend has already been somewhat busier than you expected, it's worth putting your feet up for a short while. If you still cannot bear to be seated for more than five minutes, find something to do that feeds your mind as well as strengthening your body. Family rows are best avoided now.

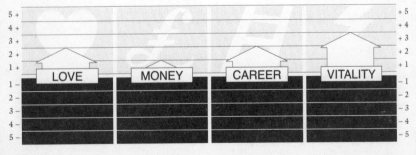

9 MONDAY
Moon Age Day 14   Moon Sign Leo

am . . . .

pm . . . .
It is towards your career and professional matters generally that your mind is encouraged to turn at the start of this particular week. There are gains to be made as a result of actions you took some time ago, and romance could be going especially well for most sons and daughters of Gemini. New contacts might prove to be very important later.

10 TUESDAY
Moon Age Day 15   Moon Sign Leo

am . . . .

pm . . . .
The present position of the Moon supports a cheerful attitude, but one that can also be emotional. Family matters are to the fore and you may be working especially hard for the sake of someone younger or less experienced than you are. Today is also ideal for lending a hand to friends.

11 WEDNESDAY
Moon Age Day 16   Moon Sign Virgo

am . . . .

pm . . . .
Trends assist you to be socially adept and able to mix with just about anyone, and you can use these traits to heighten your popularity. Of course there are always going to be people you don't like and who are not fond of you. Try as you may you can't be everyone's cup of tea – that's just the way life is, so accept it!

12 THURSDAY
Moon Age Day 17   Moon Sign Virgo

am . . . .

pm . . . .
If someone seems to be raining on your parade the advice is very simple. Keep away from them and do your own thing. Although it is fine to listen to advice, it's not so advisable to hear someone else moaning on for hours. If your attitude is that any glass is half full, you can't be responsible for people who always think it's half empty.

13 FRIDAY
Moon Age Day 18   Moon Sign Libra

am ....

pm ....
Keep up your efforts to get ahead and plan now for the weekend. Almost anyone you meet today could be that individual who has the key to success you are looking for. What should really set you apart is your enthusiasm and your zest for life. Other people notice it and want a slice of the action. Socially speaking you can ensure that life is fine.

14 SATURDAY
Moon Age Day 19   Moon Sign Libra

am ....

pm ....
A willingness to be extremely flexible might be laudable but it can also cause challenging situations. There are occasions when it is necessary to say yes or no immediately. What is more, if you refuse to commit yourself you might well annoy the very people who are presently in the best position to help you along.

15 SUNDAY
Moon Age Day 20   Moon Sign Scorpio

am ....

pm ....
A warm and contented sort of day seems to be on offer. If there isn't that much you presently want from life, you can find most of your joy in making others happy. As you do so, you can increase your own sense of contentment too. Family moments can be fun and may also bring periods of distinct nostalgia.

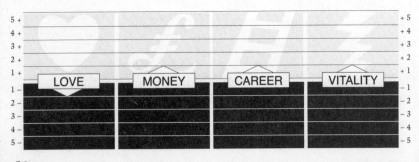

16 MONDAY
Moon Age Day 21   Moon Sign Scorpio

am . . . .

pm . . . .
Arrangements do sometimes have to be made, and it's possible that others are expecting you to make them. This won't always be easy because you have to find ways of keeping everyone happy. Be prepared to keep abreast of news and views in your locality and make the most of some project that is just about to start.

17 TUESDAY
Moon Age Day 22   Moon Sign Scorpio

am . . . .

pm . . . .
There are gains to be made on the financial front today, mostly from putting yourself in the right place at the right time. Rather than getting too hung up on details at work, it's worth taking the longer-term view whenever possible. Romance is also on the up and a new relationships could be in the offing for some Gemini people now.

18 WEDNESDAY
Moon Age Day 23   Moon Sign Sagittarius

am . . . .

pm . . . .
The middle of this week might find you a long way from your objectives but that is only your present point of view. In the Gemini life things can change in an instant and it is important for you to remain positive and optimistic. That way you will be in a position to make some major gains – but not just yet.

19 THURSDAY
Moon Age Day 24   Moon Sign Sagittarius

am . . . .

pm . . . .
Even if the lunar low seems to take the wind out of your sails, it doesn't last long and is not very potent this time around. Opt for what you know today and don't take on anything new until at least tomorrow. A favourable time to welcome someone special in your life, perhaps bringing with them a few surprises.

20 FRIDAY
Moon Age Day 25   Moon Sign Capricorn

am . . . .

pm . . . .
The lunar low is now fully out of the way and you can start progressing
positively once again. The greatest asset you presently have is your
dynamic attitude. This, together with your commitment to change,
assists you to race towards some particular objective. Sport is well
accented for Gemini.

21 SATURDAY
Moon Age Day 26   Moon Sign Capricorn

am . . . .

pm . . . .
Stop and look before you take any undue chance today because your
enthusiasm will sometimes be greater than your capabilities. There are
times when it might be best to enlist the support of someone who is an
expert in their particular field. Once you have their advice you should be
able to get ahead so much better.

22 SUNDAY
Moon Age Day 27   Moon Sign Capricorn

am . . . .

pm . . . .
There are rewarding times to be had on the social scene, but present
trends go further than this. It looks certain that you are entering the
most romantic phase of the month, so now is the time to say those special
words and to write that particular little poem that will sweep someone off
their feet. You won't believe the possible results!

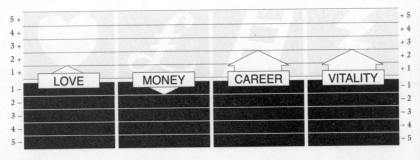

23 MONDAY
Moon Age Day 28   Moon Sign Aquarius

am . . . .

pm . . . .
If you look back across the last few weeks you should see how much further you have come than you expected. Standard responses are not enough today because you need to add to your successes by being extraordinary. Anything that makes you stand out in a crowd is grist to the mill and allows you to achieve so much more.

24 TUESDAY
Moon Age Day 29   Moon Sign Aquarius

am . . . .

pm . . . .
Encounters with others can be especially important at the moment because they allow you to review the way your own mind has been working recently. Your creative potential is favoured, so why not use this to tackle projects at home? Enlisting the support of friends would be no bad thing.

25 WEDNESDAY
Moon Age Day 0   Moon Sign Pisces

am . . . .

pm . . . .
Even if it seems that life is hard going in one way or another, you have scope to make progress, no matter how slow. That is what matters for Gemini and you only need to regroup and retrench when things have stopped altogether. Just when you think you have reached a full stop, you can begin another sentence immediately.

26 THURSDAY
Moon Age Day 1   Moon Sign Pisces

am . . . .

pm . . . .
It is true that you should not expect miracles today but that doesn't mean you can't achieve them. Most of all at the moment you need to feel needed so you may decide to give up at least some of your time to help friends. If rules get on your nerves around this time, don't be afraid to ignore them.

27 FRIDAY

Moon Age Day 2   Moon Sign Aries

am . . . .

pm . . . .
Your capacity for sound judgement is highlighted, and you can put this
to good use by offering help and advice to others. That's fine as far as it
goes but you cannot live their lives for them and in the end you need to
influence them to make their own decisions. Look out for opportunities
for a romantic fling.

28 SATURDAY

Moon Age Day 3   Moon Sign Aries

am . . . .

pm . . . .
Your intuition is more or less off the scale, which is why it may be hard
for you to put a foot wrong at present. The weekend offers you the
chance to get ahead in things you are only now trying for the first time,
and you could be discovering aptitudes you didn't know you had. You
can get others to marvel at your poise and apparent confidence.

1 SUNDAY

Moon Age Day 4   Moon Sign Aries

am . . . .

pm . . . .
Today is not a time for compromise. On the contrary, you should be sure
of your footing and needn't take no for an answer in most situations. This
could make you appear stubborn but as long as you are sure that your
actions are justified, you should carry on. Don't get too worried about
the love life of a friend but be ready with support.

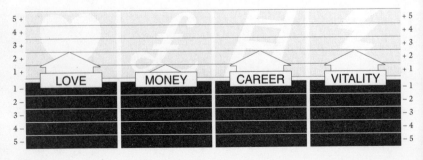

March 2009

YOUR MONTH AT A GLANCE

$\oplus$ = Opportunities are around $\ominus$ = Be on the defensive   = Life is pretty ordinary

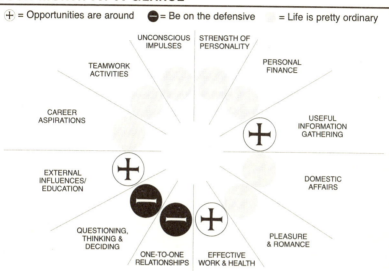

UNCONSCIOUS IMPULSES
STRENGTH OF PERSONALITY
PERSONAL FINANCE
TEAMWORK ACTIVITIES
USEFUL INFORMATION GATHERING
CAREER ASPIRATIONS
DOMESTIC AFFAIRS
EXTERNAL INFLUENCES/ EDUCATION
QUESTIONING, THINKING & DECIDING
PLEASURE & ROMANCE
ONE-TO-ONE RELATIONSHIPS
EFFECTIVE WORK & HEALTH

MARCH HIGHS AND LOWS

Here I show you how the rhythms of the Moon will affect you this month. Like the tide, your energies and abilities will rise and fall with its pattern. When it is above the centre line, go for it, when it is below, you should be resting.

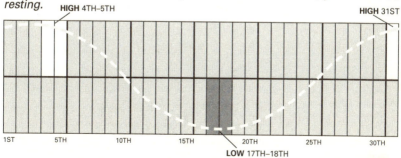

HIGH 4TH–5TH   **HIGH** 31ST

1ST   5TH   10TH   15TH   20TH   25TH   30TH

LOW 17TH–18TH

II

2 MONDAY
Moon Age Day 5   Moon Sign Taurus

am ....

pm ....
With the Moon now in your solar twelfth house things might seem slow at the beginning of this week. Don't worry though because you can soon improve matters and there are plenty of opportunities in store this week. By all means get to grips with a few necessary changes but don't put anything into action for a day or two.

3 TUESDAY
Moon Age Day 6   Moon Sign Taurus

am ....

pm ....
It is your emotional responses that seem to matter the most today. Love and romance are to the fore, encouraging you to all you can to make your partner or sweetheart feel very special. Take some time out today to decide exactly what you are going to change first tomorrow. Life has potential to get hectic!

4 WEDNESDAY
Moon Age Day 7   Moon Sign Gemini

am ....

pm ....
It's all go now and you have everything you need to make the middle of the week rather special. Energy levels are high, your intuition is strong and you needn't be held back by anything. The lunar high offers you extra chances that you shouldn't miss, and what is more it looks as though you can get your popularity going off the scale.

5 THURSDAY
Moon Age Day 8   Moon Sign Gemini

am ....

pm ....
You can continue to get life going very much your way and to take what you want without any invitation. You show yourself to be competitive and determined, though your compassion and concern for others is also very noteworthy at this time. A day to keep abreast of local news and things that are happening in and around your home.

6 FRIDAY
Moon Age Day 9   Moon Sign Cancer

am . . . .

pm . . . .
You can really set yourself apart at present by doing everything you can to help other people. Of course this is most evident in the case of relatives and friends, but that isn't the end of the story. As a Gemini you can call everyone you meet brother or sister, and this fact shows most under today's planetary trends.

7 SATURDAY
Moon Age Day 10   Moon Sign Cancer

am . . . .

pm . . . .
Life is now progressive and stable, leaving you with more time than usual to make the most of whatever the weekend has to offer. You shouldn't have to pay attention to situations for every moment of the day and can afford to relax more. Be prepared to get to grips with changes you want to make at home and enlist the support of family members.

8 SUNDAY
Moon Age Day 11   Moon Sign Leo

am . . . .

pm . . . .
If you feel that someone is not supporting you in the way you have a right to expect, you need to be tactful and diplomatic in the way you approach the situation. There could be reasons you don't yet understand and so flying off the handle now might leave you feeling somewhat foolish when you are in the picture.

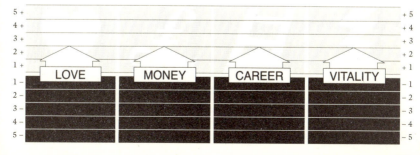

9 MONDAY   *Moon Age Day 12   Moon Sign Leo*

am . . . .

pm . . . .
The start of this particular week could be attended by a few problems,
some of which come about as a result of your association with others.
The fact is that you want to do things your own way and that may not
always be possible at the moment. A little more compromise is advisable,
together with a realisation that others can be right too.

10 TUESDAY   *Moon Age Day 13   Moon Sign Virgo*

am . . . .

pm . . . .
Co-operation should be slightly easier now, and colleagues should be in
a good position to help you out with something – that is if you are not
too proud to ask for their help. At home you can afford to show your
sweetest face to those you care about, even if one or two situations are
driving you up the wall. Patience is your best virtue now.

11 WEDNESDAY   *Moon Age Day 14   Moon Sign Virgo*

am . . . .

pm . . . .
If there is one thing that can help you now it is plain, simple logic.
Almost everyone else you come across might seem to be accepting
situations at face value, but not you. Gemini will turn over as many stones
as possible to get to the truth, and there isn't any doubt at all about your
ability to do so under present trends.

12 THURSDAY   *Moon Age Day 15   Moon Sign Libra*

am . . . .

pm . . . .
Your strength lies in cutting through the superficial to get to the heart of
any matter. With everything to play for at work there are possible
advancements in store and some Gemini people might even be thinking
about a change of career quite soon. When away from work your social
impulses are especially strong today.

13 FRIDAY
Moon Age Day 16   Moon Sign Libra

am . . . .

pm . . . .
It looks as though you are primarily motivated by your desire to succeed at all cost around this time. There is nothing wrong with this except for the fact that the price you have to pay can sometimes be too high. Let's face it, you are not a naturally ruthless person, and there probably isn't much sense in trying to pretend that you are.

14 SATURDAY
Moon Age Day 17   Moon Sign Libra

am . . . .

pm . . . .
You can easily find yourself at odds with some of the people surrounding you today, particularly if you can't agree with them how things should be done. If you really want to succeed and not fall out with anyone it might be best to work alone. An ideal time to get in touch with friends who are at a distance or who may be ill at present.

15 SUNDAY
Moon Age Day 18   Moon Sign Scorpio

am . . . .

pm . . . .
A very sociable and easy-going sort of Gemini can be put on display whilst the Moon is in Scorpio. However, you can also show great depth at present and can use this to get through to individuals who have been difficult for you to approach in the past. Your charitable instincts are especially strong at this time, and need outlets.

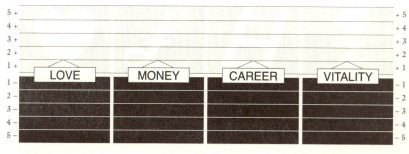

16 MONDAY
Moon Age Day 19   Moon Sign Scorpio

am . . . .

pm . . . .
It's worth putting in that extra bit of effort today so that you can get things running as smoothly as possible. That's because tomorrow and Wednesday may well be quieter and give you less chance to get ahead. If you have everything sorted today, you can afford to slow down a little during the lunar low. You can elicit plenty of support right now.

17 TUESDAY
Moon Age Day 20   Moon Sign Sagittarius

am . . . .

pm . . . .
There is really no point in pushing yourself too hard now that the lunar low has arrived. It won't make you ill or depressed but it might take the wind out of your sails regarding tasks you see as being important. If you relax, take stock and plan for the far end of the week you can avoid any undue problems and enjoy a rest.

18 WEDNESDAY
Moon Age Day 21   Moon Sign Sagittarius

am . . . .

pm . . . .
There are always people you can call on for support – that's the nature of Gemini people. Now is the time to ask for a few favours, or at least to let someone else make the running. For many this isn't easy, and the Gemini attitude is sometimes inclined to make the lunar low period far more uncomfortable than it needs to be.

19 THURSDAY
Moon Age Day 22   Moon Sign Capricorn

am . . . .

pm . . . .
Now is the time to get things back to normal – if it's possible to say what normal is for the average Gemini individual. You have scope to be sociable, chatty and very much inclined to mix business with pleasure. For some there is a chance of a new relationship or else a pepping up of one that may have flagged recently.

20 FRIDAY
Moon Age Day 23   Moon Sign Capricorn

am . . . .

pm . . . .
Personal objectives are to the fore at the moment, and you should be doing everything you can to bring your plans to fruition. There are likely to be interesting diversions on offer, and with everything to play for in the financial stakes you might also be able to ensure you are better off than you expected to be at the moment.

21 SATURDAY
Moon Age Day 24   Moon Sign Capricorn

am . . . .

pm . . . .
Look for a little more self-restraint this weekend. Even if there is plenty going on, that doesn't mean you have to try and do everything at the same time. One interest at once is the key to success now, together with co-operating with friends and family members. Steering the most diplomatic course might not be too easy today.

22 SUNDAY
Moon Age Day 25   Moon Sign Aquarius

am . . . .

pm . . . .
Keeping yourself in the picture is as important now as it ever is to the most curious and inquisitive of all the zodiac signs. The time is right to instigate new plans at home and maybe think about making yourself more comfortable in some way. Everything takes longer than it should, but that's the nature of being a Gemini.

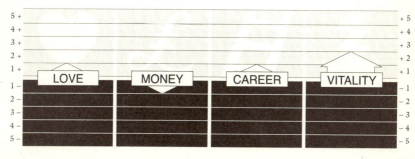

II

23 MONDAY
Moon Age Day 26   Moon Sign Aquarius

am . . . .

pm . . . .
Getting what you want right now is really a matter of being in the right place at the best time. Your intuition should tell you what to do, and it doesn't matter how much you plan because in the end you need to respond to changing circumstances. Why not get out into the fresh air and enjoy what the spring has to offer?

24 TUESDAY
Moon Age Day 27   Moon Sign Pisces

am . . . .

pm . . . .
Trends indicate that others have a much stronger influence on your thinking today than might sometimes be the case. There's nothing wrong with this, especially if you realise that what they are suggesting is based on common sense. This is a commodity that sometimes eludes you, mainly because you want to do everything as soon as possible.

25 WEDNESDAY
Moon Age Day 28   Moon Sign Pisces

am . . . .

pm . . . .
Your contribution to life is noteworthy and you can't really be a Gemini without attracting the attention of those around you. Even if most people think you are great, there are always going to be one or two individuals who don't care for your brash and cheery nature. Simply ignore these people and concentrate on everyone else.

26 THURSDAY
Moon Age Day 0   Moon Sign Pisces

am . . . .

pm . . . .
The poem goes: 'What is this life if, full of care, we have no time to stand and stare?' Nothing could be more relevant to the Gemini life because you are perpetually on the go. Sometimes this means you will miss a few of the nuances of life that make it so appealing. Be prepared to leave some time free to simply 'be' and try a little meditation.

27 FRIDAY
Moon Age Day 1   Moon Sign Aries

am . . . .

pm . . . .
Some slightly disheartening aspects to life are possible at the moment, mainly brought about as a result of the less than positive responses you are getting from others. If people seem to criticise or to see your shortcomings, maybe they have a point. Change your own perspective a little and you might come to understand their point of view.

28 SATURDAY
Moon Age Day 2   Moon Sign Aries

am . . . .

pm . . . .
You may now have access to the vitality you have been craving – but what to do with it? The fact is that you can achieve the most under present planetary trends by moving forward steadily. Since this is an unknown quantity for Gemini, it could be rather like visiting a strange country. Speaking of countries, travel is indicated soon.

29 SUNDAY
Moon Age Day 3   Moon Sign Taurus

am . . . .

pm . . . .
It's possible that not everyone is responding in the way you wish, and this is a reoccurring trend at the moment. Your best approach is to simply leave certain people to their own devices, whilst you push forward on your own. This isn't ideal for Gemini but even for you there are times when to fly solo is sensible.

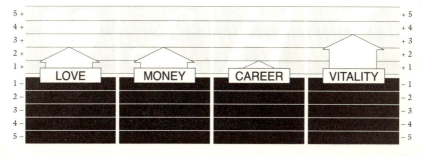

30 MONDAY
Moon Age Day 4   Moon Sign Taurus

am . . . .

pm . . . .
With the Moon now occupying your solar twelfth house you have scope
to be more contemplative than usual and also a good deal more
emotional. You can easily be brought to tears by memories of the past –
though this isn't necessarily a result of sadness. Don't worry – this rather
peculiar phase should pass very quickly.

31 TUESDAY
Moon Age Day 5   Moon Sign Gemini

am . . . .

pm . . . .
Confidence in your own abilities should now be increasing rapidly and
the lunar high also offers better luck and new incentives. Now you can
begin to show a face to the world at large that is absolutely typical of your
zodiac sign at its best. In most situations you can be funny, intelligent
and able to engage people in intelligent conversation.

1 WEDNESDAY
Moon Age Day 6   Moon Sign Gemini

am . . . .

pm . . . .
What better way to start a new month than with the lunar high assisting
you towards the conclusion of some important plans? There is no April
Fool about now as far as you are concerned, except in terms of your
heightened sense of humour and ludicrous behaviour. If Lady Luck is
paying you a visit, it pays to greet her warmly.

2 THURSDAY
Moon Age Day 7   Moon Sign Cancer

am . . . .

pm . . . .
There are signs that intimate matters need extra attention today and you
may have to work hard to see exactly why others are behaving in the way
they are. Empathy is not hard for Gemini people as a rule but when you
are running at full speed there isn't always much time for understanding.
A conscious effort is all that is required.

3 FRIDAY

Moon Age Day 8   Moon Sign Cancer

am . . . .

pm . . . .
Some of the things you are doing right now could turn out to be quite self-defeating and you need to be careful to ensure that you are not working against your best interests. If someone disagrees with you, try not to get too defensive. Keep explaining your point of view and everything should resolve itself in the end. Creative potential is highlighted.

4 SATURDAY

Moon Age Day 9   Moon Sign Leo

am . . . .

pm . . . .
The details of life don't really matter too much to the average Gemini, and it is the overview that counts. That's fine as far as it goes but there are times when you really do need to concentrate on specifics. Today is such a time and you stand most chance of succeeding in the way you want if you turn your full attention in very specific directions.

5 SUNDAY

Moon Age Day 10   Moon Sign Leo

am . . . .

pm . . . .
Financial matters could well be improving – either that or you are learning how to handle what you have in a better way. Be prepared to deal with demands from family members by listening and helping to put right matters that have gone slightly amiss. Sunday routines could turn out to be slightly tedious.

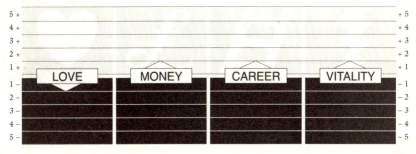

II

April 2009

YOUR MONTH AT A GLANCE

⊕ = Opportunities are around   ⊖ = Be on the defensive   = Life is pretty ordinary

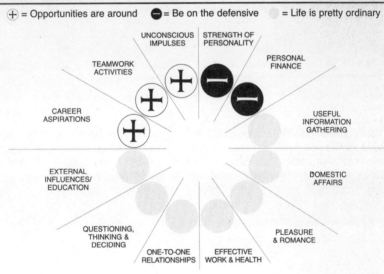

UNCONSCIOUS IMPULSES

STRENGTH OF PERSONALITY

TEAMWORK ACTIVITIES

PERSONAL FINANCE

CAREER ASPIRATIONS

USEFUL INFORMATION GATHERING

EXTERNAL INFLUENCES/ EDUCATION

DOMESTIC AFFAIRS

QUESTIONING, THINKING & DECIDING

PLEASURE & ROMANCE

ONE-TO-ONE RELATIONSHIPS

EFFECTIVE WORK & HEALTH

APRIL HIGHS AND LOWS

Here I show you how the rhythms of the Moon will affect you this month. Like the tide, your energies and abilities will rise and fall with its pattern. When it is above the centre line, go for it, when it is below, you should be resting. HIGH 1ST

HIGH 27TH–28TH

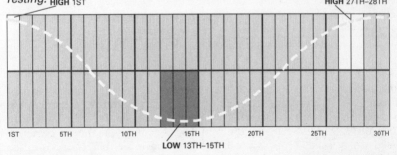

1ST   5TH   10TH   15TH   20TH   25TH   30TH

LOW 13TH–15TH

6 MONDAY
Moon Age Day 11   Moon Sign Virgo

am . . . .

pm . . . .
Your strength lies in keeping your spirits up at the beginning of this working week, and in using this time to get ahead of the herd. With plenty to play for and a generally positive attitude there is very little that you can't achieve. The one area of life that may need attention is a slightly flagging romance.

7 TUESDAY
Moon Age Day 12   Moon Sign Virgo

am . . . .

pm . . . .
There is no need to get yourself into a state regarding issues that you should be able to put right in the end. Gemini is inclined to worry about things that are sometimes inconsequential, but on the other hand you have a great capacity to look at the big picture. Don't be afraid to seek support from friends.

8 WEDNESDAY
Moon Age Day 13   Moon Sign Virgo

am . . . .

pm . . . .
Now you can renew your efforts and succeed in ways that were not open to you only a few days ago. There will probably be new incentives on offer at work, whilst at home you still have scope to make yourself more comfortable in some way. This has potential to be a busy day but one during which you can move ahead rapidly.

9 THURSDAY
Moon Age Day 14   Moon Sign Libra

am . . . .

pm . . . .
If someone close to you feels the need of greater freedom, you should be in a good position to make this a possibility. Although things may start slow during the morning by the middle of the day you should be up to speed once again. Routines can seem to be a terrible chore but are assisted if you find ways to ring the changes.

10 FRIDAY

Moon Age Day 15   Moon Sign Libra

am . . . .

pm . . . .
There's a temptation if you feel you are falling behind others in some way
to frantically do everything you can to prove yourself to colleagues and
superiors. There really is no need because people don't simply look at you
on one day. The impression you have been making of late shouldn't be
lost on those who really count.

11 SATURDAY

Moon Age Day 16   Moon Sign Scorpio

am . . . .

pm . . . .
There is much to be said for using part of the weekend to look at money
matters and to decide how you can help yourself to a greater fortune in
the longer term. In a more immediate sense there is a driving
determination to make something more for yourself regarding your
home. It looks as though more DIY could be in order!

12 SUNDAY

Moon Age Day 17   Moon Sign Scorpio

am . . . .

pm . . . .
Any small stumbling blocks today may come along in the sphere of your
social life. Perhaps things you had planned will have to be cancelled or
somehow altered at the last moment. The lunar low is just around the
corner and you may need to take account of its restricting influences for
a few hours before the Moon actually moves into Sagittarius.

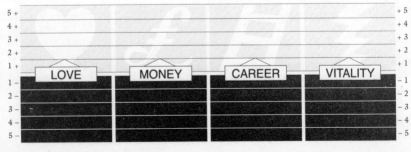

13 MONDAY
Moon Age Day 18   Moon Sign Sagittarius

am . . . .

pm . . . .
This may not be the most ambitious or potentially successful start to a working week and for that you can thank the lunar low. Not that you are prevented altogether from getting ahead. If you are willing to put in the extra effort needed, progress can still be made. On the other hand, you may decide it's easier to watch and wait.

14 TUESDAY
Moon Age Day 19   Moon Sign Sagittarius

am . . . .

pm . . . .
Your best response to any frustrations that crop up today is to allow life to flow over you rather than trying to swim against the tide. Unfortunately that isn't your way and all the advice in the world won't prevent you from trying that much harder. Be prepared to deal with the moods of others.

15 WEDNESDAY
Moon Age Day 20   Moon Sign Sagittarius

am . . . .

pm . . . .
Although the Moon is still in Sagittarius as today gets started, it doesn't stay there much beyond lunchtime. The difference when it moves should be quite apparent, even if it is more in your head than in the sky. You can get people to react more positively and once again move your plans forward at a significant speed.

16 THURSDAY
Moon Age Day 21   Moon Sign Capricorn

am . . . .

pm . . . .
There could well be much more energy available today – though in reality you are simply getting back to normal. Your cheerful and optimistic approach to life can have a profound influence on those around you, and you have scope to persuade people to put themselves out wholesale on your behalf. A good time to ask for favours.

17 FRIDAY
Moon Age Day 22   Moon Sign Capricorn

am . . . .

pm . . . .
The more imaginative you can be today, the greater are the incentives that are on offer. Chances are that you can also make use of creative trends to beautify your surroundings, either at home or at work. When things look good you work and react more positively, so it's important to get things right.

18 SATURDAY
Moon Age Day 23   Moon Sign Aquarius

am . . . .

pm . . . .
When it comes to the social side of life you shouldn't need many invitations in order to get involved. You love to be around people who are happy and forward-looking and should willingly get involved in new possibilities at the moment. Keep an eye open for advantages that come from people living far away or working at a distance.

19 SUNDAY
Moon Age Day 24   Moon Sign Aquarius

am . . . .

pm . . . .
Your potential for success is increased at the moment thanks to the position of the planet Mars in your chart. Although fiery Mars also supports a more go-getting approach, it does offer you the chance to prove yourself in a number of different ways. In romantic situations you can prove yourself to be a real charmer today.

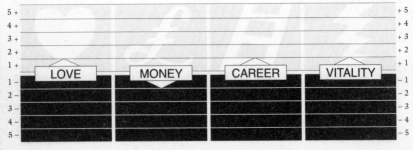

20 MONDAY   *Moon Age Day 25   Moon Sign Aquarius*

am . . . .

pm . . . .
It is towards money that your mind is encouraged to turn on a number of occasions during April and today is no exception. The time is right to make certain that you will be as comfortable as you would wish in the long-term future, and to be inventive when planning ahead. At home you may need extra patience today.

21 TUESDAY   *Moon Age Day 26   Moon Sign Pisces*

am . . . .

pm . . . .
Even if there isn't quite as much success about as you would wish when it comes to the practical side of life, in terms of social matters and personal attachments you can make progress. You can't make ground in every area of your life at the same time, so be content that you can get at least some aspects going your way.

22 WEDNESDAY   *Moon Age Day 27   Moon Sign Pisces*

am . . . .

pm . . . .
Getting to grips with any disputes in your family or friendship circle could prove to be a real nuisance on a day when you need all your energy to focus on getting ahead in a practical sense. If you simply cannot make others see eye-to-eye, in the end you might decide to leave them to get on with it.

23 THURSDAY   *Moon Age Day 28   Moon Sign Aries*

am . . . .

pm . . . .
For a few planetary reasons you won't suffer fools gladly today and may well become highly irritated with people who walk into the same mistakes time and time again. This may be more evident in the case of friends who simply won't learn that trawling the same old ground in a relationship sense is only causing them more and more pain.

24 FRIDAY

Moon Age Day 29   Moon Sign Aries

am . . . .

pm . . . .
Outwardly you can appear very calm, even on those occasions when you are shaking like mad inside. This ability is especially enhanced at present, allowing you to appear to be far more confident than is actually the case. Since you can fool almost anyone, get on and show just how capable and unflappable you seem to be!

25 SATURDAY

Moon Age Day 0   Moon Sign Taurus

am . . . .

pm . . . .
Something may seem to be missing today, particularly if other people are not doing what is expected of them. Give a little nudge if necessary but don't push things too much. In the end you may decide that it is simply easier to get on and do things on your own. An ideal day to mix with those you don't see too often.

26 SUNDAY

Moon Age Day 1   Moon Sign Taurus

am . . . .

pm . . . .
Getting to exactly where you want to be may not be all that easy today, mainly because the Moon is passing through your solar twelfth house. You can change everything tomorrow when the lunar high comes along, but for the moment it's worth biding your time. Romance is emphasised for the evening.

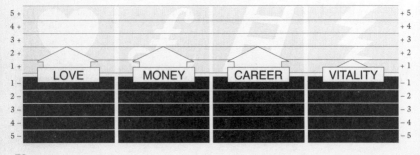

27 MONDAY

Moon Age Day 2   Moon Sign Gemini

am . . . .

pm . . . .

The Moon is back in Gemini and this is the part of the month when you really do need to be using all that energy and determination. Progress is the order of the day and you shouldn't take no for an answer when it comes to getting your own way. There is better luck available and you have the ability to get most things right first time.

28 TUESDAY

Moon Age Day 3   Moon Sign Gemini

am . . . .

pm . . . .

The trivia of life shouldn't matter at all today if you are pushing forward on all fronts and refusing to be diverted by irrelevant details. Not only are you able to feather your own nest but you have scope to stick up for those who don't have quite the level of drive that comes as second nature to you. Be prepared to make new starts in relationships.

29 WEDNESDAY

Moon Age Day 4   Moon Sign Cancer

am . . . .

pm . . . .

Your best resonse to feeling touchy and reluctant about certain issues today is to seek the support of colleagues or friends in order to get ahead. All day long there are likely to be small irritations and the sort of delays that can really get on your nerves. Instead of reacting to such situations, you would be wise to stay cool, calm and relaxed.

30 THURSDAY

Moon Age Day 5   Moon Sign Cancer

am . . . .

pm . . . .

Love and romantic issues now have potential to be highly rewarding and this is the area of life that is highlighted the most between now and the weekend. Concerns regarding work are best put on hold because you can't concentrate on everything at the same time. A day to let new personalities have a bearing on your life big time.

1 FRIDAY

Moon Age Day 6   Moon Sign Cancer

am . . . .

pm . . . .
Even if you are generally happy in social situations, it may be that certain people are not doing all they could to put you at your ease. Maybe the time has come to speak out and at the very least to let people know if they are coming across as rude or overbearing. You can do this without causing rows.

2 SATURDAY

Moon Age Day 7   Moon Sign Leo

am . . . .

pm . . . .
Many of you will be away from work for the weekend, but this need not prevent you from getting on famously in almost anything you decide to undertake. They say a change is as good as a rest, and that certainly seems to be the case as far as you are concerned. Amongst your many interests today, you can afford to find time for family members.

3 SUNDAY

Moon Age Day 8   Moon Sign Leo

am . . . .

pm . . . .
Trends suggest a less practical Gemini at the moment, particularly if your mind is creative and somehow distracted. That means that certain things probably won't get done, or else they will take much longer than usual. It might be best to avoid routines and to go off on a trip or a shopping spree with people you like.

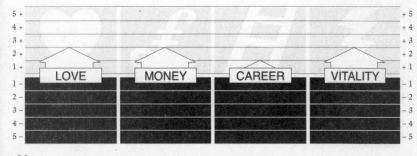

May

2009

YOUR MONTH AT A GLANCE

$\oplus$ = Opportunities are around $\ominus$ = Be on the defensive   ◯ = Life is pretty ordinary

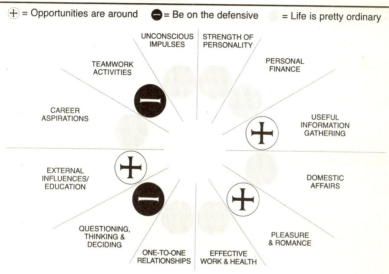

UNCONSCIOUS IMPULSES

STRENGTH OF PERSONALITY

TEAMWORK ACTIVITIES

PERSONAL FINANCE

CAREER ASPIRATIONS

USEFUL INFORMATION GATHERING

EXTERNAL INFLUENCES/ EDUCATION

DOMESTIC AFFAIRS

QUESTIONING, THINKING & DECIDING

PLEASURE & ROMANCE

ONE-TO-ONE RELATIONSHIPS

EFFECTIVE WORK & HEALTH

MAY HIGHS AND LOWS

Here I show you how the rhythms of the Moon will affect you this month. Like the tide, your energies and abilities will rise and fall with its pattern. When it is above the centre line, go for it, when it is below, you should be resting.

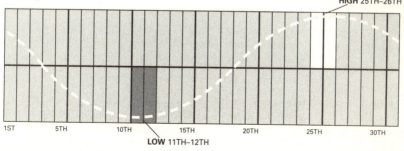

HIGH 25TH–26TH

1ST   5TH   10TH   15TH   20TH   25TH   30TH

LOW 11TH–12TH

4 MONDAY
Moon Age Day 9   Moon Sign Virgo

am . . . .

pm . . . .
You might need to be a little careful over details today. It's possible that not everyone is as organised as you are, and instead of just looking at what you are doing, it's also worth taking account of the actions of others. In a personal sense you have scope to be generally happy and to enjoy fruitful and rewarding relationships.

5 TUESDAY
Moon Age Day 10   Moon Sign Virgo

am . . . .

pm . . . .
If necessary you have what it takes to be quite dominant and forceful today, though not with people who are having problems. You are still able to account for the actions of others but to do so constantly can prove to be rather frustrating. An early start might help – that way you will leave more time later to do whatever you wish.

6 WEDNESDAY
Moon Age Day 11   Moon Sign Libra

am . . . .

pm . . . .
With plenty of mental energy at your disposal you can deal quickly with issues that prove troublesome to colleagues and friends. In addition to getting on well at work, trends also support finding ways and means to enjoy yourself more in a social sense. The Sun is moving rapidly towards the part of the sky that suits you the best.

7 THURSDAY
☿   *Moon Age Day 12   Moon Sign Libra*

am . . . .

pm . . . .
Wherever possible today you need to focus on practical goals and will be at your best when getting on with things that show a positive and quick result. Frustration is possible if life doesn't go your way and if you are forced to slow down too much. Socially speaking, today offers a chance to be full of beans!

8 FRIDAY   ☿   *Moon Age Day 13   Moon Sign Scorpio*

am . . . .

pm . . . .
Both today and across the weekend you have everything you need to
achieve positive results, no matter what you decide to do. A quieter spell
is possible at the beginning of next week so it might be sensible to do
whatever you need at work now. That way you won't feel harassed or
rushed when Monday comes along.

9 SATURDAY   ☿   *Moon Age Day 14   Moon Sign Scorpio*

am . . . .

pm . . . .
The focus is on a socially motivated sort of weekend and a chance to get
away from ordinary matters as much as you can. The weather is
improving and the call of the great outdoors is probably very noticeable
within your nature now. When it comes to getting on well in groups you
rarely have any problems, and shouldn't have now.

10 SUNDAY   ☿   *Moon Age Day 15   Moon Sign Scorpio*

am . . . .

pm . . . .
This should be the sort of Sunday when you pick and mix freely from
life's selection. Spending time with loved ones or with friends could be
appealing, and you should avoid taking on more than you have to in a
practical sense. Jobs in and around your home are fine but do make sure
you leave some hours free for simple enjoyment.

5 +				+ 5
4 +				+ 4
3 +				+ 3
2 +				+ 2
1 +				+ 1
LOVE	MONEY	CAREER	VITALITY
1 -				- 1
2 -				- 2
3 -				- 3
4 -				- 4
5 -				- 5

11 MONDAY ☿ *Moon Age Day 16   Moon Sign Sagittarius*

am . . . .

pm . . . .
It is unlikely that today will turn out to be the most dynamic or successful start to any working week that you have experienced so far this year. The lunar low encourages you to slow down your reactions and makes some jobs seem like walking through treacle. A day to let others take the decisions, whilst you watch, wait and prepare yourself for later.

12 TUESDAY ☿ *Moon Age Day 17   Moon Sign Sagittarius*

am . . . .

pm . . . .
Even if some of your energy has disappeared, you needn't let your sense of humour go missing. On the contrary you are able to make others laugh, and that lifts your spirits too. Be prepared to call on the good offices of an expert, perhaps to do with your car or some domestic gadget. Stay cool, calm and collected.

13 WEDNESDAY ☿ *Moon Age Day 18   Moon Sign Capricorn*

am . . . .

pm . . . .
You can make this a much better day from the very moment it commences. Get out of bed expecting to succeed and that is what is likely to happen. There are people about at the moment who are in an excellent position to help you get something you really want. What matters is the way you approach them, so turn on that Gemini charm.

14 THURSDAY ☿ *Moon Age Day 19   Moon Sign Capricorn*

am . . . .

pm . . . .
In a career sense you can afford to do things your own way and needn't stand for much in the way of interference. There is no point at all falling out with those you may have to rely on later, so it would be best to bite your tongue on occasions. Why not find a place to daydream at some stage today? It does you good!

15 FRIDAY ☿ *Moon Age Day 20 Moon Sign Capricorn*

am . . . .

pm . . . .
There is a slight danger today that you will act first and ask questions later. This is not at all unusual for Gemini people, especially younger ones, but it doesn't always work to your advantage. A more circumspect attitude and slower actions can sometimes get you what you want much more effectively than impatience.

16 SATURDAY ☿ *Moon Age Day 21 Moon Sign Aquarius*

am . . . .

pm . . . .
In some situations, and especially ones to do with home and family, trends indicate a more circumspect approach in which you are inclined to delay decisions. This is why others find you difficult to understand. Just when they think they have you taped as someone who can't wait five minutes, off you go into a prolonged period of contemplation.

17 SUNDAY ☿ *Moon Age Day 22 Moon Sign Aquarius*

am . . . .

pm . . . .
Trends are very promising as far as love and romance are concerned. All relationships look rewarding, but especially those that have a touch of Cupid about them. There are strong advantages for Gemini people who are working today but your sense of freedom is so marked right now that any feeling of being fettered probably won't be tolerated.

LOVE MONEY CAREER VITALITY

18 MONDAY ☿ *Moon Age Day 23   Moon Sign Pisces*

am . . . .

pm . . . .
Along comes a period that should be excellent for business and for any
sort of financial investment. With a combination of intuition and
common sense you can get through or round any obstacles that life
throws in your path, and can remain confident and happy throughout
most of today.

19 TUESDAY ☿ *Moon Age Day 24   Moon Sign Pisces*

am . . . .

pm . . . .
An ideal time to give what you can to those who are not so fortunate as
you are. It is very important right now that you show what a very
charitable individual you can be. This is for your own peace of mind but
also because you can use it to impress someone special. There might be
slight drawbacks at work, perhaps caused by difficult colleagues.

20 WEDNESDAY ☿ *Moon Age Day 25   Moon Sign Aries*

am . . . .

pm . . . .
Your need for new experiences is just about as strong as it gets – and
that's saying something in the case of Gemini. You needn't be tied down
by anyone or anything and can show a positive response to any sort of
adventure. This would be a good day to take a complete break or even to
embark on a holiday if that were possible.

21 THURSDAY ☿ *Moon Age Day 26   Moon Sign Aries*

am . . . .

pm . . . .
It may not always be easy today to see someone else's point of view, so
be prepared to work hard in order to avoid losing your temper. Even if it
seems as if everyone you meet is determined to be stupid, the fact is that
you are not at your most patient. Try to calm down and if possible to
laugh at your own impetuosity.

22 FRIDAY ☿ *Moon Age Day 27   Moon Sign Aries*

am . . . .

pm . . . .

As a Gemini you are usually good with others, but present trends suggest a spell in which people annoy you all the time. This won't last long and once the Moon moves into Taurus later today you can get back to your old self. Tedious tasks need to be handled with care but leave time later in the evening for yourself.

23 SATURDAY ☿ *Moon Age Day 28   Moon Sign Taurus*

am . . . .

pm . . . .

Your need for fresh fields and pastures new is now stronger than ever, yet at the same time you have scope to be deep and contemplative this weekend. For this you can thank the Moon in your solar twelfth house. Conflicting thoughts pass through your mind and getting yourself into a really positive frame of mind may not be at all easy.

24 SUNDAY ☿ *Moon Age Day 0   Moon Sign Taurus*

am . . . .

pm . . . .

Your strength lies in being more settled in your attitude and much more willing to listen to those around you. Family members can be a source of great joy and you should be doing all you can to support those you care for. Once again you become the team player that Gemini naturally is and can show people your sunny and cheerful disposition.

	LOVE	MONEY	CAREER	VITALITY

25 MONDAY ☿ *Moon Age Day 1   Moon Sign Gemini*

am . . . .

pm . . . .
The Moon moves into Gemini just at the right time for you to start a new
working week with all the enthusiasm and determination you can muster.
Make the most of situations that are definitely going your way and do
what you can to show how capable you are. A few timely investments
now should pay great dividends later.

26 TUESDAY ☿ *Moon Age Day 2   Moon Sign Gemini*

am . . . .

pm . . . .
It's good to start anything new today and to move forward with both
enthusiasm and a very optimistic attitude. Getting to the bottom of a
specific mystery will require getting your detective head on right now.
Don't be afraid to stretch yourself mentally and physically at this stage of
the month.

27 WEDNESDAY ☿ *Moon Age Day 3   Moon Sign Cancer*

am . . . .

pm . . . .
Now is the time to show the fun side of your personality to everyone and
make a joke of situations that a few days ago would have really wound
you up. In almost every way you display the very best of your zodiac sign
and as a result your popularity is not in doubt. In particular, you have
scope to make the most of romance.

28 THURSDAY ☿ *Moon Age Day 4   Moon Sign Cancer*

am . . . .

pm . . . .
You get the very best from most situations by being light-hearted and fun
to have around. The time is right to show others your personality and
demonstrate that you are fascinating and intelligent. What really sets you
apart is that you know a little about everything and so shouldn't be stuck,
no matter what company you are in.

29 FRIDAY ☿ *Moon Age Day 5   Moon Sign Leo*

am . . . .

pm . . . .
Trends support a growing excitement about the prospects that stand before you. Plan now for long-distance travel and for holidays that are not so far into the future. In the shorter term you will need change and diversity during the coming weekend, so why not do something about it right now?

30 SATURDAY ☿ *Moon Age Day 6   Moon Sign Leo*

am . . . .

pm . . . .
What you definitely don't need today is to feel that you are hemmed in by circumstances and by tasks that you hate. Your best approach is to ring the changes whenever possible, and if that means leaving some jobs until later then so be it. Who knows? Whilst you are not looking someone kind might come along and do some of them for you!

31 SUNDAY ☿ *Moon Age Day 7   Moon Sign Virgo*

am . . . .

pm . . . .
It's worth concentrating your energies as much as possible today on having fun and being in the company of people you really like. Standard responses to family members probably won't work too well and you will have to be just a little more imaginative in the way you deal with loved ones generally. Romance is well accented today.

LOVE   MONEY   CAREER   VITALITY

June 2009

YOUR MONTH AT A GLANCE

⊕ = Opportunities are around   ⊖ = Be on the defensive   ⚪ = Life is pretty ordinary

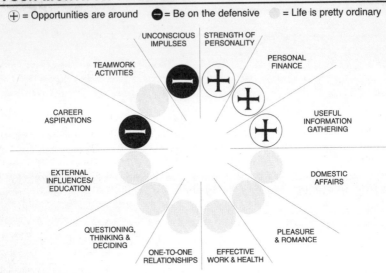

- UNCONSCIOUS IMPULSES
- STRENGTH OF PERSONALITY
- PERSONAL FINANCE
- TEAMWORK ACTIVITIES
- USEFUL INFORMATION GATHERING
- CAREER ASPIRATIONS
- EXTERNAL INFLUENCES/ EDUCATION
- DOMESTIC AFFAIRS
- QUESTIONING, THINKING & DECIDING
- PLEASURE & ROMANCE
- ONE-TO-ONE RELATIONSHIPS
- EFFECTIVE WORK & HEALTH

JUNE HIGHS AND LOWS

Here I show you how the rhythms of the Moon will affect you this month. Like the tide, your energies and abilities will rise and fall with its pattern. When it is above the centre line, go for it, when it is below, you should be resting.

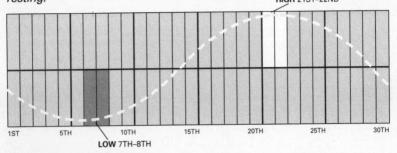

HIGH 21ST–22ND

1ST   5TH   10TH   15TH   20TH   25TH   30TH

LOW 7TH–8TH

1 MONDAY

Moon Age Day 8   Moon Sign Virgo

am . . . .

pm . . . .
If you feel there isn't enough going on in your life at the very beginning of June you can afford to step up your own actions and turn your imagination up to full. The Sun is now in your solar first house and that makes this the time of the year during which you can give your very best. Energy is well starred.

2 TUESDAY

Moon Age Day 9   Moon Sign Libra

am . . . .

pm . . . .
Action and exercise come under the spotlight. Whilst others are slowing down and taking stock, you should be pushing forward in the most progressive way. This could cause the odd problem and if people can't keep up you may have to proceed on your own. It's time to give your best in sporting activities or when extra energy is needed.

3 WEDNESDAY

Moon Age Day 10   Moon Sign Libra

am . . . .

pm . . . .
Things you hear on the grapevine today could prove to be very important so it is necessary that you keep your ears open and listen in on all possible conversations. Even if details get in the way of fast progress, you can still get where you want to be. Nothing will slow you down for long, and others could marvel at your tenacity.

4 THURSDAY

Moon Age Day 11   Moon Sign Scorpio

am . . . .

pm . . . .
What really sets you apart at the moment is how good you are at negotiating. If the country needed a new diplomat you should be up for the job. You can use this trait to pour oil on troubled waters in the case of friends or colleagues who argue, and to get on well with anyone who has been very awkward in the past.

5 FRIDAY
Moon Age Day 12   Moon Sign Scorpio

am . . . .

pm . . . .
There isn't much doubt that you can put yourself in the limelight both today and across the weekend. How could people generally fail to recognise that you are around? You show yourself to be cheerful and enterprising, which gets you noticed. What is more, you have ways and means of bringing the shyest people out of their shells.

6 SATURDAY
Moon Age Day 13   Moon Sign Scorpio

am . . . .

pm . . . .
Be prepared to get out of the house and find somewhere beautiful to be this weekend. If that isn't possible spend time in the garden or read books about far-off and exotic places. In one way or another your mind needs diversion. You have a sense of freedom that is stronger than at any time this year. What an excellent time this would be for a holiday!

7 SUNDAY
Moon Age Day 14   Moon Sign Sagittarius

am . . . .

pm . . . .
It may not be easy to hide your feelings or emotions with the lunar low around. If you feel something you are inclined to say it before you have time to think. This could get you into a little hot water, but most people will respect your honesty. Even if starting jobs is easy today, it might be slightly more difficult to finish them.

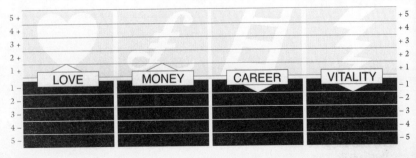

8 MONDAY   *Moon Age Day 15   Moon Sign Sagittarius*

am . . . .

pm . . . .
Now is the best time of the month to gather together those pieces of information that are going to be useful to you later on. You have a naturally inquisitive mind and this may well be working overtime at the moment. Rather than getting dragged down by inconsequential worries at the moment, it's worth concentrating on the positive side of life.

9 TUESDAY   *Moon Age Day 16   Moon Sign Capricorn*

am . . . .

pm . . . .
The lunar low is now out of the way and this allows you to move forward more progressively and in the certain knowledge that you know what you are doing. There may still be people around who seem to want to throw a spanner in the works, but you can see clearly how to get round difficulties. Rely the most on your own judgement now.

10 WEDNESDAY   *Moon Age Day 17   Moon Sign Capricorn*

am . . . .

pm . . . .
You certainly won't lack strength when it comes to doing what you know is right, but there is a slight potential here for causing yourself some difficulties. Maybe you should be willing to compromise more today, because that way you can respond better to changing circumstances and awkward people.

11 THURSDAY   *Moon Age Day 18   Moon Sign Capricorn*

am . . . .

pm . . . .
As far as your overall popularity is concerned, you have what it takes to make sure that you are number one in many people's estimation. This allows you to take a few advantages that you might normally miss and to be generally happier about yourself. Colleagues could be especially accommodating at this time.

12 FRIDAY
Moon Age Day 19   Moon Sign Aquarius

am . . . .

pm . . . .
Your strength lies in taking control, especially when it comes to money matters. Now is the time to capitalise on general good luck and to push through to the winning post when faced with situations of conflict. There are possible arguments about but these can be toned down.

13 SATURDAY
Moon Age Day 20   Moon Sign Aquarius

am . . . .

pm . . . .
Venus is now in your solar first house and this helps you to find all the golden words you need when dealing with affairs of the heart. Few people are naturally more poetic than Gemini, and you could charm the birds from the very trees whilst Venus occupies this position. You also have what it takes to conquer a particular fear today.

14 SUNDAY
Moon Age Day 21   Moon Sign Pisces

am . . . .

pm . . . .
Mars is also presently in your solar first house, which gives an edge to your nature and encourages you to be naturally competitive and even slightly more aggressive than usual in some situations. The combination of planetary positions for you at this time shows how well you curb your more pushy side but yet still get your own way.

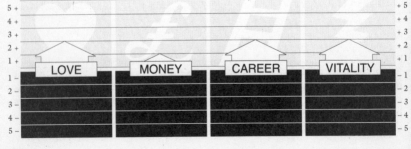

15 MONDAY

Moon Age Day 22   Moon Sign Pisces

am . . . .

pm . . . .

There is the possibility that you will be invited to state your case as far as issues at work are concerned, and even if what you have to say is very much to the point, it might not be quite as diplomatic as usual. In one way that's no bad thing because there are certain things that simply have to be said. Be prepared to sugar the pill a little though.

16 TUESDAY

Moon Age Day 23   Moon Sign Pisces

am . . . .

pm . . . .

There are details to deal with today and maybe little time to fit in everything you want to do. Although it might seem to slow you up it would be sensible to write yourself a list early in the day and to get things sorted out properly in your mind. That way you avoid repeating yourself later and can be sure that everything will get done.

17 WEDNESDAY

Moon Age Day 24   Moon Sign Aries

am . . . .

pm . . . .

Routines can be the scourge of your life around now. The fact is that the Sun remains in your solar first house and this highlights freedom and personal choice. If people and situations try to change that by tying you down to anything, frustration may follow. All the same you would be wise to keep your temper.

18 THURSDAY

Moon Age Day 25   Moon Sign Aries

am . . . .

pm . . . .

With better support now available, you should be able to push ahead more, though some care is still necessary when you are dealing with other people. Your attitude can be quite forthright and you could give some offence without realising. What you don't need is to spend hours putting things right that shouldn't have gone wrong at all.

19 FRIDAY
Moon Age Day 26   Moon Sign Taurus

am . . . .

pm . . . .
Things can now be quietened down a little ahead of the lunar high. This is the time of the month when the Moon occupies your solar twelfth house, encouraging you to be more contemplative and also more emotional. Getting to grips with the genuine needs of family members and your partner ought to be a piece of cake today and tomorrow.

20 SATURDAY
Moon Age Day 27   Moon Sign Taurus

am . . . .

pm . . . .
A day to get things sorted out and be especially busy in and around your home. If you want to make your life more comfortable, this is the time to start planning your moves. You have what it takes to persuade family members to be compliant and friends to be accommodating.

21 SUNDAY
Moon Age Day 28   Moon Sign Gemini

am . . . .

pm . . . .
The lunar high supports a very jolly frame of mind in which you are happy to join in anything that sounds like fun. Energy levels will be especially well marked and you are able to cut through red tape as if it didn't exist at all. It's worth getting in touch with your best friends today and if possible arranging some sort of outing or treat.

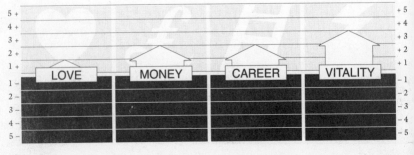

96

22 MONDAY
Moon Age Day 29   Moon Sign Gemini

am . . . .

pm . . . .

You can achieve a very positive start to the new working week because the lunar high is still doing you many favours. You know exactly what you want from life and will show just how keen you are to help others on the way. Money matters might be on your mind, but you are able to deal with these as easily as you accommodate everything else.

23 TUESDAY
Moon Age Day 0   Moon Sign Cancer

am . . . .

pm . . . .

Your desire to break the bounds of the possible has rarely been more emphasised than it is right now. Instead of rushing into things you need to take stock first, to avoid unnecessary work. Although you are presently very keen you might not be quite as organised as usual. Seeking some sound advice later would be no bad thing.

24 WEDNESDAY
Moon Age Day 1   Moon Sign Cancer

am . . . .

pm . . . .

You can afford to remain generally assertive, though that isn't necessarily the best way to be under present trends. The softer and more thoughtful your approach turns out to be, the greater can be the rewards later. By all means be willing to defend yourself, though not before you have been attacked. More patience is a must.

25 THURSDAY
Moon Age Day 2   Moon Sign Leo

am . . . .

pm . . . .

There are times at present when it would simply be easier to ask for what you want, instead of trying to alter situations in other ways. You show a tendency to go around the houses instead of taking direct routes and you may marvel at this propensity later. Why not get on side with those people who you know instinctively can help you out?

II

26 FRIDAY
Moon Age Day 3   Moon Sign Leo

am . . . .

pm . . . .
Be prepared to listen if others tell you exactly what they think. Although this might sometimes come as a shock it's best that you know because then you can deal with issues instead of letting them simmer away below the surface. In some situations you may still be rushing headlong to nowhere in particular.

27 SATURDAY
Moon Age Day 4   Moon Sign Virgo

am . . . .

pm . . . .
The weekend is here again and there should be plenty of opportunities about for enjoyment at all sorts of levels. Try not to take on too much in the way of work this weekend if you can avoid doing so because a holiday frame of mind works best. A day to spend time with your partner and family members and find ways to entertain them.

28 SUNDAY
Moon Age Day 5   Moon Sign Virgo

am . . . .

pm . . . .
There may not be too much time for comfort today, particularly if you remain active and energetic. It is possible to do a thousand things in the time it might sometimes take you to do ten, but of course there is a price to pay. By the time you go to bed you could be absolutely exhausted, so do pace yourself.

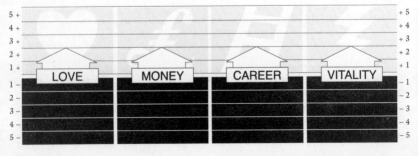

29 MONDAY

Moon Age Day 6   Moon Sign Libra

am . . . .

pm . . . .
If you aren't in the best frame of mind to face too many home truths today, it's worth avoiding heart-to-heart conversations. Trends suggest that your ego may be slightly more fragile than an egg at the moment and you will easily be hurt by offhand comments. You may decide to spend at least some time on your own today.

30 TUESDAY

Moon Age Day 7   Moon Sign Libra

am . . . .

pm . . . .
The Sun is now in your solar second house, heralding a practical interlude. Sorting out finances is not only necessary now but is assisted by trends. It doesn't matter how many details you have to deal with because you can sort them out easily and show an understanding of matters that would confuse others.

1 WEDNESDAY

Moon Age Day 8   Moon Sign Libra

am . . . .

pm . . . .
As July gets started, you can afford to be raring to go and to face all sorts of tests that might frighten you on occasions. Your forthright but fair manner can enable you to make some new friends and everything is set for a strongly romantic period. Impressing your partner or sweetheart is as easy as simply being yourself.

2 THURSDAY

Moon Age Day 9   Moon Sign Scorpio

am . . . .

pm . . . .
The activity continues and there is room for you to be as busy as ever for much of today and tomorrow. In amongst all you have to do, new ideas should be starting to crystallize in your mind and these can be put to good use in only a few days. Rather than rushing your fences in career matters, be willing to sort out your plans before you react.

3 FRIDAY
Moon Age Day 10   Moon Sign Scorpio

am . . . .

pm . . . .
Although the start of today can be as hectic as the last few days, as the hours pass so you may decide to slow down markedly. For this you can thank the changing position of the Moon, which is now moving into your opposite zodiac sign of Sagittarius. Two days under much slower trends are at hand.

4 SATURDAY
Moon Age Day 11   Moon Sign Sagittarius

am . . . .

pm . . . .
You probably won't have all the answers today, no matter how hard you decide to look for them. In most areas of life it might be better to accept that this is a time to recharge your batteries, though romance can still go ahead at a pace. The choice is yours. Either relax and enjoy the ride or else keep pushing against obstacles.

5 SUNDAY
Moon Age Day 12   Moon Sign Sagittarius

am . . . .

pm . . . .
There isn't much chance of you being in the social limelight today but if that is not where you would wish to be at the moment, that shouldn't be much of a problem. Now is the time to sort out new ideas and to keep your mind ticking over. Leave fresh starts until tomorrow or the day after.

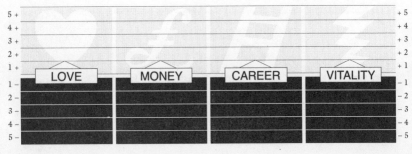

100

July 2009

YOUR MONTH AT A GLANCE

+ = Opportunities are around   − = Be on the defensive   = Life is pretty ordinary

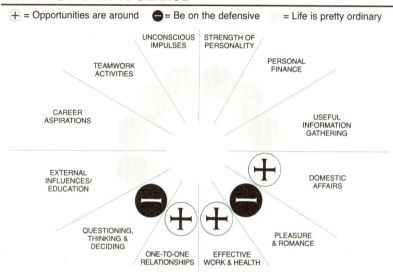

UNCONSCIOUS IMPULSES
STRENGTH OF PERSONALITY
TEAMWORK ACTIVITIES
PERSONAL FINANCE
CAREER ASPIRATIONS
USEFUL INFORMATION GATHERING
EXTERNAL INFLUENCES/ EDUCATION
DOMESTIC AFFAIRS
QUESTIONING, THINKING & DECIDING
PLEASURE & ROMANCE
ONE-TO-ONE RELATIONSHIPS
EFFECTIVE WORK & HEALTH

JULY HIGHS AND LOWS

Here I show you how the rhythms of the Moon will affect you this month. Like the tide, your energies and abilities will rise and fall with its pattern. When it is above the centre line, go for it, when it is below, you should be resting.

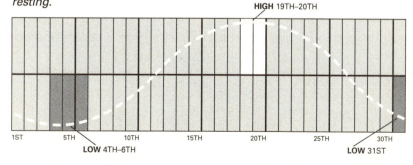

HIGH 19TH–20TH

1ST   5TH   10TH   15TH   20TH   25TH   30TH

LOW 4TH–6TH

LOW 31ST

101

6 MONDAY
Moon Age Day 13   Moon Sign Sagittarius

am . . . .

pm . . . .
With Mercury now placed in your second house you should have little difficulty in getting your message across to others in a positive way. Of course you do have to contend with the lunar low at the moment and that could throw the odd spanner in the works. By tomorrow you should be fully up and running again.

7 TUESDAY
Moon Age Day 14   Moon Sign Capricorn

am . . . .

pm . . . .
Emotional responses may be a little squashed by the present position of Mars and it might not be too easy to find the right words when you are dealing with someone in the family or possibly your partner. Trends relating to money matters are more positive, offering you scope to strengthen your finances during this week.

8 WEDNESDAY
Moon Age Day 15   Moon Sign Capricorn

am . . . .

pm . . . .
The time is right to apply your considered approach to improving your financial situation. Maybe you should be pursuing promotion at work or reaping the benefits of efforts you put in previously. Socially speaking you should be on great form.

9 THURSDAY
Moon Age Day 16   Moon Sign Aquarius

am . . . .

pm . . . .
By all means spend time today with people who seem to know what they are talking about, but be a little careful because all that glistens probably isn't gold. Gemini is not a generally cautious zodiac sign and there are times when you ignore your own common sense. Get-rich-quick schemes or people with a bad past reputation are best avoided.

10 FRIDAY *Moon Age Day 17   Moon Sign Aquarius*

am . . . .

pm . . . .
It isn't that you lack enterprise or initiative at present, but when it comes to the killer instinct you just don't seem to have it. This is a temporary state of affairs caused by the position of Mars in your solar twelfth house. It won't be long before you find yourself well able to put a full stop to deals of any sort. It's worth seeking help from friends.

11 SATURDAY *Moon Age Day 18   Moon Sign Aquarius*

am . . . .

pm . . . .
Gemini is invariably popular and you can certainly ensure that this will be the case across the weekend. There may be the odd person who doesn't take to you and sometimes this happens because Gemini is inclined to attract a little jealousy from less gregarious types. A family outing or a shopping spree might suit you well today.

12 SUNDAY *Moon Age Day 19   Moon Sign Pisces*

am . . . .

pm . . . .
If you are on holiday at the moment, or simply taking a day or two away, you have chosen very wisely. There is a good mix in your nature right now. On the one hand you can enjoy boisterous moments and knock-about situations, but you also have what it takes to fully appreciate beautiful places, historic buildings or fine art.

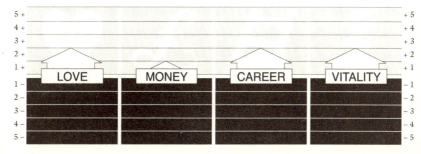

13 MONDAY
Moon Age Day 20   Moon Sign Pisces

am . . . .

pm . . . .
Managing your own resources is best today and there are moments when you need to look carefully at the decisions you are making. It might be best not to part with cash early this week unless you are certain that you will be getting value for money. Later in the week the trends support a wiser Gemini who is less easy to catch out.

14 TUESDAY
Moon Age Day 21   Moon Sign Aries

am . . . .

pm . . . .
Your best asset is generally your ability to get on well with just about anyone. You know how to approach people and don't have to think through any sort of strategy as a rule because this skill is instinctive. Use it to the full today. Even if you have had problems with someone in the past, be prepared to give it another go and expect to succeed.

15 WEDNESDAY
Moon Age Day 22   Moon Sign Aries

am . . . .

pm . . . .
If there is something you really want from life, now is one of those times when you need to go out and get it. There are gains to be made from simply being in the right place at the best time, and although the road to success sometimes seems to be very long and quite tortuous, you should gradually be getting where you need to be.

16 THURSDAY
Moon Age Day 23   Moon Sign Taurus

am . . . .

pm . . . .
A slightly quieter time is on offer as the Moon passes through your solar twelfth house. This doesn't require you to withdraw from life in any way but it can make you less inclined to be pushy or to believe you have all the answers. You will certainly be in the market for listening to what others have to say, which may be no bad thing.

17 FRIDAY
Moon Age Day 24   Moon Sign Taurus

am . . . .

pm . . . .
Look carefully at your diary today in case you have missed, or are about
to miss, an important birthday or anniversary. The Gemini life is an
extremely busy one and you don't always take note of events that are very
important – to others if not to you. A belated greeting could well be in
order.

18 SATURDAY
Moon Age Day 25   Moon Sign Taurus

am . . . .

pm . . . .
Even if things are still not running as fast as you might wish, you can
change that tomorrow. For the moment enjoy a fairly sedate pace and
revel in the successes of family members and friends. Socially speaking
you should be on great form. An ideal time to show others that you are
interesting, intelligent and above all funny.

19 SUNDAY
Moon Age Day 26   Moon Sign Gemini

am . . . .

pm . . . .
With Sunday comes the lunar high, though it's full force only shows if
you happen to work today. It is towards potential success in both business
and your personal life that your mind is now encouraged to turn.
Capitalise on greater luck, a better belief in your own abilities and
support from others. The aspects are positive, so use them!

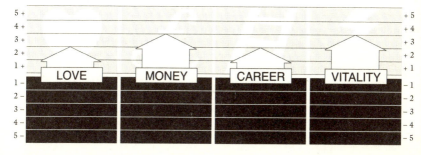

20 MONDAY
Moon Age Day 27   Moon Sign Gemini

am . . . .

pm . . . .
Today should suit you down to the ground. You have what it takes to turn heads and to impress people when it really matters. When it comes to romance you might be surprised by the responses that you can attract and you may be so popular in a general sense that people will refuse you virtually nothing.

21 TUESDAY
Moon Age Day 28   Moon Sign Cancer

am . . . .

pm . . . .
It shouldn't be hard for you to juggle many different situations at the same time – in fact to do so is second nature. This isn't the case for everyone though, and you could have friends or colleagues in a terrible state if they find it difficult to keep up with you. Be prepared to slow down long enough to explain your strategy – that is if you have one.

22 WEDNESDAY
Moon Age Day 0   Moon Sign Cancer

am . . . .

pm . . . .
Venus is now in your solar first house and that has to be good as far as romance is concerned. You have what it takes to be kind, considerate and extremely sexy. No wonder you can get people falling over themselves to get to know you better. That's fine if you are in the market for a new romance but could be embarrassing otherwise.

23 THURSDAY
Moon Age Day 1   Moon Sign Leo

am . . . .

pm . . . .
The Sun has now moved into your solar third house from where it has a great part to play in your actions out there in the wide world. You should begin to relish any sort of challenge even more than usual and won't have any difficulty getting on with powerful and influential people. Dull people probably won't interest you at all.

24 FRIDAY
Moon Age Day 2   Moon Sign Leo

am . . . .

pm . . . .
There are some very enriching experiences available at the moment and many of these come as a result of your magnetic personality and your ability to be in the right place at the best possible time. You may not get everything you want from life at the moment but can come quite close on occasions. The weekend ahead can be quite exciting.

25 SATURDAY
Moon Age Day 3   Moon Sign Virgo

am . . . .

pm . . . .
Romance is to the fore at this time and the weekend offers much in terms of personal attachments. Family concerns could well be taking up at least some of your time and there are gains to be made from simply listening to what loved ones have to say. This sounds easy enough, but you don't always pay enough attention.

26 SUNDAY
Moon Age Day 4   Moon Sign Virgo

am . . . .

pm . . . .
Trends assisst you to stretch yourself somehow, since you can easily become bored if nothing specific is happening around you. That's why it is so important for you to take command. A reappraisal of your personal finances would be no bad thing, and you could be slightly better off than you expected to be.

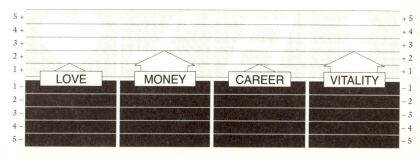

27 MONDAY
Moon Age Day 5   Moon Sign Libra

am . . . .

pm . . . .
Although Gemini is usually a team player you might get on better today
if you take command and maybe even work on your own. It's not that
you doubt the integrity or ability of others, simply that you need to be
certain of your ground at present and want to make sure everything goes
well. A few timely explanations might be necessary.

28 TUESDAY
Moon Age Day 6   Moon Sign Libra

am . . . .

pm . . . .
Positive responses from those you work with could help you to make
today go with a certain swing, but there might still be those who refuse
to accept that you are number one for the moment. Use a little tact and
diplomacy, both of which you have in great abundance if you choose to
turn them on. You can avoid trouble if you do.

29 WEDNESDAY
Moon Age Day 7   Moon Sign Scorpio

am . . . .

pm . . . .
The pace of life should be increasing rapidly and in some ways it could
be too fast, even for you. If people try to push you into situations for
which you are not ready – or never will be ready – don't be afraid to apply
the brakes. Now is the time to get to grips with jobs at home and to plan
for a journey or even a holiday that is coming soon.

30 THURSDAY
Moon Age Day 8   Moon Sign Scorpio

am . . . .

pm . . . .
This is one of the few days of this month when you could get something
for nothing. It is therefore vital that you keep your eyes open today
because you might lose out and kick yourself later. By all means try new
sports or activities now but don't expect to be in the mood for them
during the next couple of days. Quieter times are in store.

31 FRIDAY
Moon Age Day 9   Moon Sign Sagittarius

am . . . .

pm . . . .
The lunar low offers a chance to be more contemplative and to remove yourself from all situations of conflict or places that are hectic. You need time to recharge flagging batteries and this is more vital for Gemini than for just about any other zodiac sign. It might be hard to explain your inner feelings now.

1 SATURDAY
Moon Age Day 10   Moon Sign Sagittarius

am . . . .

pm . . . .
When it comes to practical concerns you would be wise to leave matters to others to sort out today. Although you remain basically capable you may not have your usual patience and in any case you want to spend more time on your own. Confidence is not exactly absent at the moment, but you aren't in your usual 'up for anything' frame of mind.

2 SUNDAY
Moon Age Day 11   Moon Sign Sagittarius

am . . . .

pm . . . .
Today is a game of two halves. During the morning you may be quite withdrawn and less inclined to join in but early in the afternoon the Moon moves out of Sagittarius and into Capricorn. When this happens it should be as if a veil is lifted from you. Everything can be exciting again and your social life will be the winner.

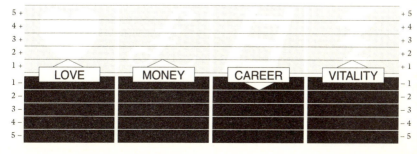

August 2009

YOUR MONTH AT A GLANCE

$\oplus$ = Opportunities are around ⚫ = Be on the defensive ⚪ = Life is pretty ordinary

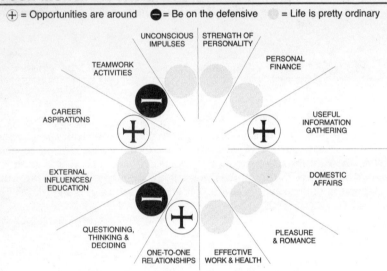

AUGUST HIGHS AND LOWS

Here I show you how the rhythms of the Moon will affect you this month. Like the tide, your energies and abilities will rise and fall with its pattern. When it is above the centre line, go for it, when it is below, you should be resting.

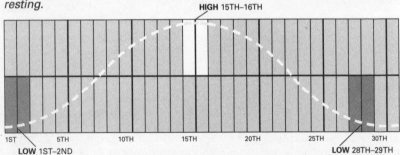

3 MONDAY
Moon Age Day 12   Moon Sign Capricorn

am . . . .

pm . . . .
Venus is in your second house, encouraging a slightly standoffish aproach when dealing with others at a one-to-one level. This isn't the way you intend to be and those who know you the best are unlikely to take offence. Confidence to do the right thing at work remains strong and you show yourself to be capable.

4 TUESDAY
Moon Age Day 13   Moon Sign Capricorn

am . . . .

pm . . . .
It is still early in the week but nevertheless you have sufficient energy available to work hard all day and to dance all night if necessary. You have what it takes to make things go your way to a greater extent than during the last few days, though in reality your efforts were always well starred.

5 WEDNESDAY
Moon Age Day 14   Moon Sign Aquarius

am . . . .

pm . . . .
Be prepared for everyone to demand your attention at the same time. Though this is not particularly unusual for your zodiac sign you could run out of steam by the middle of the afternoon. Stamina is something you don't usually lack, but you needn't get paranoid about being tired. A good sleep is all you need, so why not try to have an early night?

6 THURSDAY
Moon Age Day 15   Moon Sign Aquarius

am . . . .

pm . . . .
Gemini people can be terrible hypochondriacs and if you are now more prone than usual to aches, pains or little infections, you will probably think you are terribly ill. Of course if in doubt you should seek medical advice, but you have to bear in mind that you are one of life's natural actors and so being dramatic is second nature to you.

7 FRIDAY
Moon Age Day 16   Moon Sign Aquarius

am . . . .

pm . . . .
When it comes to getting on well with just about anyone you come across, today could not be better. At heart you are a very kind person. True you can sometimes be slightly thoughtless but the word 'malice' doesn't enter your personal vocabulary. Now is the time to show just how much you care and to do so in very practical ways.

8 SATURDAY
Moon Age Day 17   Moon Sign Pisces

am . . . .

pm . . . .
The weekend may well arrive more quickly than you expected, particularly if you have been busy and occupied of late. You have scope to find ways to have fun and to do what you can to inspire younger family members. An excursion of some sort might suit you fine, perhaps in the company of people who are really important.

9 SUNDAY
Moon Age Day 18   Moon Sign Pisces

am . . . .

pm . . . .
You have potential to be on fine form today, and the most important aspect of your nature at present is that you are so funny. If people are happy to be with you, you can really gain in confidence. Your world now is a mutual appreciation society because you can afford to give as many compliments as you receive.

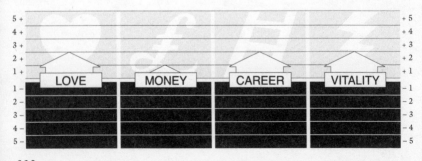

10 MONDAY
Moon Age Day 19   Moon Sign Aries

am . . . .

pm . . . .
Don't be surprised if things are going in your favour today. Arrangements you made earlier can now start to pay off and your level of co-operation with colleagues is noteworthy. Beware of getting too cocky about recent success or you could find that you have to start something all over again. Balance is required now.

11 TUESDAY
Moon Age Day 20   Moon Sign Aries

am . . . .

pm . . . .
You have what it takes to be the centre of attention at present, though there isn't anything especially unusual about that for a Gemini individual. The only slight problem with being in the limelight is that you have to be on your best behaviour. Looking right is also important, so it's worth reviewing your wardrobe!

12 WEDNESDAY
Moon Age Day 21   Moon Sign Aries

am . . . .

pm . . . .
Even if plans have to be altered at short notice, that need not be too much of a problem because you tend to think on your feet most of the time. There might not be quite as much order in your life as you would presently wish but you do have the ability to sort things out, even if those around you definitely do not.

13 THURSDAY
Moon Age Day 22   Moon Sign Taurus

am . . . .

pm . . . .
Don't be afraid to speak your mind today, even though you may not be in a particularly argumentative frame of mind. With the Moon in your twelfth house, part of you is constantly saying 'anything for a peaceful life' but on the other hand you know you can't leave certain issues for long. You can persuade people to be responsive.

14 FRIDAY
Moon Age Day 23   Moon Sign Taurus

am . . . .

pm . . . .
A day to sort out finances and prepare to make progress from tomorrow onwards. If there is anything routine that needs sorting out, today is the time to get on with it. For the next few days you might be busy across the board and probably won't have time for the minutiae of life that you can address right now.

15 SATURDAY
Moon Age Day 24   Moon Sign Gemini

am . . . .

pm . . . .
The Moon is back in your zodiac sign and the time to have fun has arrived. The lunar high coincides with the weekend and that offers you scope to enjoy yourself and to have fun in the company of people with whom you get on well. If you have been off colour of late, you may well be feeling a good deal better now.

16 SUNDAY
Moon Age Day 25   Moon Sign Gemini

am . . . .

pm . . . .
Don't be afraid to take the odd chance. Fortune favours the bold and this is particularly true in your case today. If you have time on your hands that you can spend doing things that please you, you can make today a short holiday. Why not leave routine jobs until later and take people along with you on an exciting jaunt?

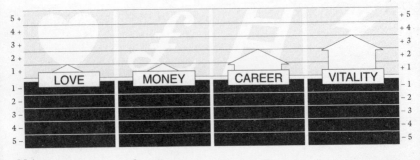

17 MONDAY
Moon Age Day 26   Moon Sign Cancer

am . . . .

pm . . . .
The Moon is in your solar second house at the moment, supporting well considered and quite sensible opinions. Not that everyone thinks so. There are colleagues or associates who may consider your present ideas to be quite odd. Your job today is to find ways and means of talking them round.

18 TUESDAY
Moon Age Day 27   Moon Sign Cancer

am . . . .

pm . . . .
There may be a short interlude at the moment during which you will be concentrating rather less on professional matters and somewhat more on home and what it means. You might be especially comfortable amongst loved ones just now, leading you to seek the sense of security that can come from simply being in the bosom of your family.

19 WEDNESDAY
Moon Age Day 28   Moon Sign Leo

am . . . .

pm . . . .
Now you have scope to push forward again, perhaps more progressively than has been the case for quite some time. Even if you are no more energetic or determined, you can be more organised and that is what seems to make the difference. A few details necessary to your success in the long-term future are best sorted out now.

20 THURSDAY
Moon Age Day 0   Moon Sign Leo

am . . . .

pm . . . .
Mercury is presently in your solar fourth house, highlighting your commitment towards your home and family. This is even reflected in the way you talk, and communications with loved ones can be especially warm and sincere. Your confidence is boosted all the time under present planetary trends.

Ⅱ

21 FRIDAY
Moon Age Day 1   Moon Sign Virgo

am . . . .

pm . . . .
Although there may be pressures from the outside world that get to you around this time, in the main you can afford to be fairly content with your lot and still spend time with those you care about the most. Your commitment to the wider world may not be quite as noteworthy as usually is the case.

22 SATURDAY
Moon Age Day 2   Moon Sign Virgo

am . . . .

pm . . . .
It's worth being a little circumspect now before you spend large amounts of money. It isn't that you are likely to be cheated – simply that you may be able to get a better bargain if you are willing to look around. Today is ideal for spending as much time as possible with your partner. If you don't have one, maybe you should be looking.

23 SUNDAY
Moon Age Day 3   Moon Sign Libra

am . . . .

pm . . . .
A fun time is on offer for many sons and daughters of Gemini. With everything to play for and a great sense of joy in your heart it is easy for you to have a positive influence on the world at large. Keep up with the actions and thoughts of friends, one or two of which could have a great part to play in your own life in the days and weeks ahead.

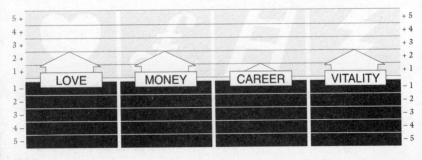

24 MONDAY
Moon Age Day 4   Moon Sign Libra

am . . . .

pm . . . .
The Sun has now entered your solar fourth house and this means that in a general sense for the next month the focus is on your family circumstances and your home. Don't be afraid to spend less time thinking about your career or social life and more hours in the company of relatives. Avoid unnecessary concerns today.

25 TUESDAY
Moon Age Day 5   Moon Sign Scorpio

am . . . .

pm . . . .
It's important to be in the know today and in the right place to benefit yourself financially. Make the most of conversations with those who are in a position to offer sound advice, and of opportunities to take on your resources. New hobbies or pastimes could well be on your mind.

26 WEDNESDAY
Moon Age Day 6   Moon Sign Scorpio

am . . . .

pm . . . .
For once you should manage to stay as cool as a cucumber, even if everyone else in your vicinity is in the middle of a panic. Your confidence level remains high and you can be especially good whenever you are in the public eye. Getting others to notice you means being on your best behaviour at all times – well nearly all times!

27 THURSDAY
Moon Age Day 7   Moon Sign Scorpio

am . . . .

pm . . . .
Most Gemini subjects should be able to keep things ticking along quite nicely, and even if you don't win the lottery this week, you might also be feeling fairly lucky. Be prepared to be up with the lark and enjoying the very best that the summer can deliver. An unexpected break isn't out of the question.

28 FRIDAY

Moon Age Day 8   Moon Sign Sagittarius

am . . . .

pm . . . .
For two days you may well be more withdrawn and less inclined to pit
your wits against the world at large. The lunar low this time will bring a
period of some isolation when you might be quite happy with your own
company for much of the time. There is nothing depressing about this
period. You are simply choosing to be quieter.

29 SATURDAY

Moon Age Day 9   Moon Sign Sagittarius

am . . . .

pm . . . .
The start of the weekend may not bring much in the way of excitement,
for which you could be quite grateful. The lunar low supports staying
indoors or at least not wandering very far from home. Although you
might feel very slightly out of sorts it will be difficult to pinpoint exactly
what might be wrong.

30 SUNDAY

Moon Age Day 10   Moon Sign Capricorn

am . . . .

pm . . . .
A more bustling and active period is now on offer as soon as the Moon
leaves Sagittarius. That could well make it feel as though you are
suddenly shooting forward at breakneck speed when in fact you are
simply reverting to your normal Gemini life. The emphasis is on loving
words and commitment to home.

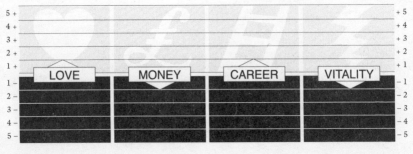

31 MONDAY   *Moon Age Day 11   Moon Sign Capricorn*

am . . . .

pm . . . .
You would be wise to be fairly circumspect at the start of this particular week, otherwise you might speak out too soon and get yourself into a degree of hot water. The more you think about things first, the less likely it will be that you cause problems for yourself. It's worth seeking ideas about travel from friends.

1 TUESDAY   *Moon Age Day 12   Moon Sign Capricorn*

am . . . .

pm . . . .
Even if you remain generally committed to the domestic sphere of life this is one day on which your career might predominate. This is also an ideal time for making arrangements concerning educational matters. Don't forget a family birthday or some sort of anniversary. It's important to others.

2 WEDNESDAY   *Moon Age Day 13   Moon Sign Aquarius*

am . . . .

pm . . . .
Trends support a need to feel warm and protected at the moment. Even if you aren't off colour, some insecurity is possible. This is par for the course as far as Gemini is concerned and all you need are a few words of reassurance from people who really matter. Avoid unnecessary details at work.

3 THURSDAY   *Moon Age Day 14   Moon Sign Aquarius*

am . . . .

pm . . . .
What you are thinking and the words you use to express yourself might be at odds with each other right now. The fact is that you want to be more truthful but you fear that a touch of diplomacy would work best. This is very wise of you. In the end you can sort things out fully but would be sensible to sugar the pill – at least for now.

4 FRIDAY

Moon Age Day 15   Moon Sign Pisces

am . . . .

pm . . . .
Your usual urge to be part of a group is less pronounced, except in the
case of family groups, which remain especially important for now. With
the weekend in sight you should plan now for some excursion or treat
that would please your partner no end and which could turn out to be
fun for you too. Finances can be strengthened today.

5 SATURDAY

Moon Age Day 16   Moon Sign Pisces

am . . . .

pm . . . .
With a slight relaxation of some tension you can bring fun and games
galore to this weekend. The teasing side of your nature is enhanced, and
people generally love it when you are in such a good frame of mind. Be
prepared to welcome new personalities into your life and to make the
most of their input.

6 SUNDAY

Moon Age Day 17   Moon Sign Pisces

am . . . .

pm . . . .
The Sun in your solar fourth house encourages you to gear much of what
you do right now towards the happiness and security of others. You
needn't push yourself especially hard and should find endless hours to
spend in happy situations. What pleases you the most today is simply to
talk to people you find fascinating.

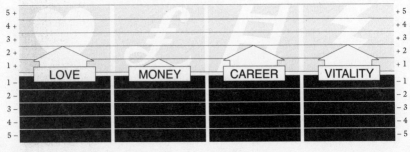

September
2009

YOUR MONTH AT A GLANCE

⊕ = Opportunities are around   ⊖ = Be on the defensive   = Life is pretty ordinary

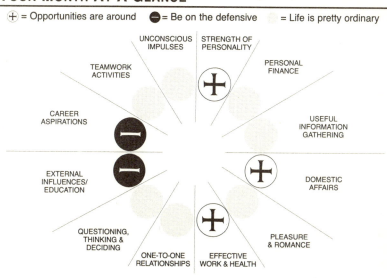

SEPTEMBER HIGHS AND LOWS

Here I show you how the rhythms of the Moon will affect you this month. Like the tide, your energies and abilities will rise and fall with its pattern. When it is above the centre line, go for it, when it is below, you should be resting.

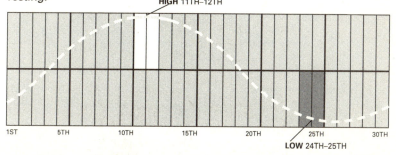

7 MONDAY ☿ *Moon Age Day 18   Moon Sign Aries*

am . . . .

pm . . . .
What might set today apart is the feeling that you have the time to do
whatever takes your fancy. It's worth making sure that your schedule isn't
rushed at the moment, so that you can get to grips with situations that
have been waiting in the wings. On the financial front you need to be
careful, but can still spend.

8 TUESDAY ☿ *Moon Age Day 19   Moon Sign Aries*

am . . . .

pm . . . .
The present position of the Sun puts the emphasis on things you can do
to make your home life more comfortable. Be imaginative, because this
trend does not simply mean redecorating the living room. What has been
wrong with family attachments? Is a new understanding necessary? It's
time to act.

9 WEDNESDAY ☿ *Moon Age Day 20   Moon Sign Taurus*

am . . . .

pm . . . .
Stand by to make this a slightly steadier sort of day, and be aware that
emotional matters are highlighted. People's situations can really move
your heart and you may decide to take on some commitments that will
form at least a part of your life for a long time to come.

10 THURSDAY ☿ *Moon Age Day 21   Moon Sign Taurus*

am . . . .

pm . . . .
There should now be plenty of time available to think before you act. For
a Gemini this has to be a good thing because you are generally so inclined
to simply launch yourself into any sort of situation with a kind of
abandon. It is especially important around now to analyse financial needs
before you commit yourself to wholesale spending.

11 FRIDAY ☿ *Moon Age Day 22   Moon Sign Gemini*

am . . . .

pm . . . .

The time is right to act. Instead of accepting what others are saying and reacting accordingly, you now have what it takes to make the choices for yourself. With everything stacked in your favour some sort of coup could be achieveable, and you are so astute and quick with the lunar high around you can leave others guessing.

12 SATURDAY ☿ *Moon Age Day 23   Moon Sign Gemini*

am . . . .

pm . . . .

Things still look positive, even if the arrival of the weekend has put a temporary halt to your professional aspirations. Now you have a chance to turn your attention towards personal attachments and especially in the direction of romance. It's time to sweep someone off their feet and to show just how caring and committed you are.

13 SUNDAY ☿ *Moon Age Day 24   Moon Sign Cancer*

am . . . .

pm . . . .

There are signs that people will be happy to have you around and are unlikely to question either your motives or the decisions you make. Don't be afraid to take the lead, even if it is only in terms of social situations. The autumn is approaching, so why not get out there and enjoy what this most beautiful season has to offer?

LOVE	MONEY	CAREER	VITALITY

14 MONDAY ☿ *Moon Age Day 25   Moon Sign Cancer*

am . . . .

pm . . . .
Directness is the key in situations where you are face to face with other people. Even if you are naturally inclined to talk others round over a fairly long period, this may not work under present planetary trends. Your best approach is to tell it how it is, even if this goes against the grain for one or two individuals.

15 TUESDAY ☿ *Moon Age Day 26   Moon Sign Leo*

am . . . .

pm . . . .
Venus remains in your solar third house and that assists you to be especially silver-tongued when it comes to finding words of love to heap upon that most important person. An ideal day to make a real fuss of family members who have achieved success, and to do whatever you can to make those around you feel warm and wanted.

16 WEDNESDAY ☿ *Moon Age Day 27   Moon Sign Leo*

am . . . .

pm . . . .
It might feel as though something remains undone today – even if you cannot put your finger on what that might be. A state of anticipation such as this should come as no surprise to you because it is a regular visitor to Gemini. Think carefully about just how well you can contribute to social situations now.

17 THURSDAY ☿ *Moon Age Day 28   Moon Sign Virgo*

am . . . .

pm . . . .
Mercury has now moved on in your solar chart and from its present position supports a slightly more circumspect approach for a while. Your thought processes remain as quick as ever but you may now be more inclined to bite your tongue before you speak out. This can be a real boon on occasions and could avoid you making some mistakes.

18 FRIDAY   ☿   *Moon Age Day 29   Moon Sign Virgo*

am . . . .

pm . . . .
With the Moon in your solar fourth house you have what it takes to be
companionable and very sensitive to others. Your chief concern may be
those you love at home, but there are other influences to show just how
hard you are still working. There is more than a touch of the genius
about the way you handle things.

19 SATURDAY   ☿   *Moon Age Day 0   Moon Sign Virgo*

am . . . .

pm . . . .
The focus is on your desire to know more and more, which could lead
you up some unexpected roads today, turning over stones wherever you
go. There won't always be an end gain to your present curiosity. It's
simply the sort of person you are. However, in the fullness of time you
can ensure that everything you learn has a use in your life.

20 SUNDAY   ☿   *Moon Age Day 1   Moon Sign Libra*

am . . . .

pm . . . .
Venus remains strong in your chart and still enhances your ability to be
poetic and deeply romantic. You could charm the birds from the trees at
present and have everything you need to make a conquest. An ideal time
to welcome someone you haven't seen for quite some time back into
your life.

	LOVE	MONEY	CAREER	VITALITY

21 MONDAY ☿ *Moon Age Day 2 Moon Sign Libra*

am . . . .

pm . . . .
Decision-making can be made easier if you can persuade other people to follow your lead. This may even extend to certain individuals who certainly haven't listened to your point of view so avidly in the past. You might even become slightly suspicious, but the sort of reactions you can attract should be honest and genuine.

22 TUESDAY ☿ *Moon Age Day 3 Moon Sign Scorpio*

am . . . .

pm . . . .
If you keep up the momentum for the moment, you can make sure there is time enough to rest later in the week. Turn on all your intuition and let this be your guide, particularly with people who are naturally very deep and difficult to fathom. Common sense is important but it can only take you so far.

23 WEDNESDAY ☿ *Moon Age Day 4 Moon Sign Scorpio*

am . . . .

pm . . . .
It should be easy to take the right decision in a work sense, though perhaps more difficult to know what to do domestically or romantically. Maybe you should have a chat with a friend, preferably a member of the opposite sex. You can then make use of opinions that would never have occurred to you on your side of the gender divide.

24 THURSDAY ☿ *Moon Age Day 5 Moon Sign Sagittarius*

am . . . .

pm . . . .
Now comes the time to take things slower and to be willing to hide in the shadows just a little. Decisions you make and actions you take could be too impulsive, which is why you may decide to make and take as few as possible. Confidence takes a short holiday but at least you know it shouldn't last longer than a couple of days.

25 FRIDAY   ☿   *Moon Age Day 6   Moon Sign Sagittarius*

am . . . .

pm . . . .
With the lunar low still around it could feel as if you are carrying a heavy
burden today. Actually nothing has changed except your attitude, and all
that is really required is some patience. By tomorrow you can get right
back on form, and what look like mountains before you now will have
shrunk to the size of molehills.

26 SATURDAY   ☿   *Moon Age Day 7   Moon Sign Capricorn*

am . . . .

pm . . . .
The Moon occupies a position this weekend that offers you scope to
move closer to family members, in both an emotional and a practical
sense. If there are family outings to be enjoyed, make sure that you join
in as much as possible. You may still have things on your mind but these
are only as real as the morning mist.

27 SUNDAY   ☿   *Moon Age Day 8   Moon Sign Capricorn*

am . . . .

pm . . . .
Although you may still not be quite as committed to life in the fast lane
as would normally be the case, you are able to look ahead and plan your
next moves. A fairly quiet sort of Sunday might appeal to you and if it is
within your power to turn down the volume of commitment and activity,
there's much to be said for doing so.

	LOVE	MONEY	CAREER	VITALITY
5 +				+ 5
4 +				+ 4
3 +				+ 3
2 +				+ 2
1 +				+ 1
1 -				- 1
2 -				- 2
3 -				- 3
4 -				- 4
5 -				- 5

28 MONDAY ☿ *Moon Age Day 9   Moon Sign Capricorn*

am . . . .

pm . . . .
Mars is now in your solar second house, encouraging any anger to smoulder rather than burst into flame. In the main a passive approach works best, but that doesn't mean letting people put on you. Adversaries will certainly come unstuck if they underestimate your potential reaction.

29 TUESDAY ☿ *Moon Age Day 10   Moon Sign Aquarius*

am . . . .

pm . . . . , ...
Mercury and Venus both now occupy your solar fourth house, placing the emphasis on your commitment to family members and your home environment. Not only are you able to think about domestic situations but you can live them much more than busy Gemini often would. Decisions may be necessary.

30 WEDNESDAY ☿ *Moon Age Day 11   Moon Sign Aquarius*

am . . . .

pm . . . .
Be prepared to look towards fulfilling as many practical objectives as you can today because in certain areas you may be falling behind your own targets. In particular you need to show colleagues and superiors that you are committed and fully in gear. It is likely to be the things you say rather than what you do that counts for the most at present.

1 THURSDAY *Moon Age Day 12   Moon Sign Pisces*

am . . . .

pm . . . .
At the start of a new month you might be panicking about some commitment that is around the corner. It is best for Gemini not to worry too much in advance of situations but rather to make certain that everything is in place. After that you can afford to relax and turn your attention in other directions. You work hard and fast now.

2 FRIDAY

Moon Age Day 13   Moon Sign Pisces

am . . . .

pm . . . .
Getting what you want from life today is merely a case of opening your mouth and asking for it. A little cheek can go a very long way and you can use your natural charm to make sure people don't refuse your requests. New possessions that come to you around this time might not be quite as appealing as you thought they would be.

3 SATURDAY

Moon Age Day 14   Moon Sign Pisces

am . . . .

pm . . . .
A day to put your faith in people you know to be both reliable and honest. It isn't often that Gemini is duped by quick-talk and a slick attitude but you might be at present. There are people in the world who are even better than you at making a silk purse out of a sow's ear, and it's worth looking out for them around this time.

4 SUNDAY

Moon Age Day 15   Moon Sign Aries

am . . . .

pm . . . .
There is still a very strong commitment to matters of hearth and home. Although the position of the Sun is urging you to take part in events that are out there in the world at large, that fourth-house Venus is still holding you back. Try to be flexible today and listen to what is on offer before you commit yourself to any specific course of action.

	LOVE	MONEY	CAREER	VITALITY

Octuber
2009

YOUR MONTH AT A GLANCE

⊕ = Opportunities are around   ⊖ = Be on the defensive   = Life is pretty ordinary

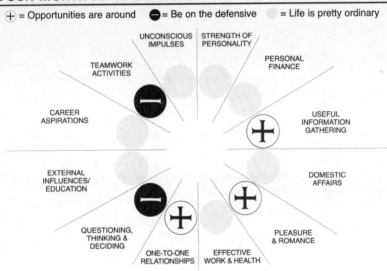

OCTOBER HIGHS AND LOWS

Here I show you how the rhythms of the Moon will affect you this month. Like the tide, your energies and abilities will rise and fall with its pattern. When it is above the centre line, go for it, when it is below, you should be resting.

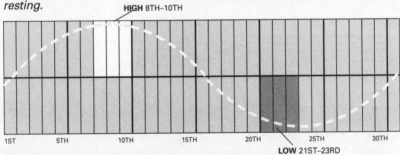

5 MONDAY
Moon Age Day 16   Moon Sign Aries

am . . . .

pm . . . .
There should be no shortage of tasks to get your teeth into at the start
of this week, and trends emphasise a desire to get everything possible
done. Of course there may be moments when you have to stop and think
more clearly about specific issues and so rushing all the time could prove
to be a negative approach.

6 TUESDAY
Moon Age Day 17   Moon Sign Taurus

am . . . .

pm . . . .
You may still need to be fairly circumspect in some regards, and there
could also be a slight tendency to worry over family members and certain
situations at home. Issues that you normally deal with easily might prove
to be slightly upsetting whilst the Moon occupies your solar twelfth
house, but these are only temporary hiccups.

7 WEDNESDAY
Moon Age Day 18   Moon Sign Taurus

am . . . .

pm . . . .
If you give yourself fully to one task at once you can ensure things turn
out just fine. What you don't need at this time is to have to start jobs all
over again because they were not done properly. It's possible you are
being monitored at present, and will give a better impression of yourself
if it is seen that you are efficient and exacting.

8 THURSDAY
Moon Age Day 19   Moon Sign Gemini

am . . . .

pm . . . .
Now the whole situation changes and you can push ahead on a number
of different fronts. The lunar high assists you to be generally carefree and
happy to take advantage of any small opportunity that comes your way.
When you need a leg up you can persuade others to oblige, and in social
settings you should be truly charming.

9 FRIDAY
Moon Age Day 20   Moon Sign Gemini

am . . . .

pm . . . .
There isn't much doubt about the power of your intuition today and you
can afford to gamble a little more than might usually be the case. Those
inner thoughts that bubble to the surface all day allow you to realise facts
that didn't occur to you before. It may also be possible to spend a little
more than you thought would be likely at this time.

10 SATURDAY
Moon Age Day 21   Moon Sign Gemini

am . . . .

pm . . . .
A mixture of tact and absolute confidence makes your approach to others
so good that they could hardly refuse you any reasonable request. As a
result this is the best day of the week to ask for something you want –
maybe a rise in salary or different working conditions. In any situation
where you are explaining yourself, you should positively shine.

11 SUNDAY
Moon Age Day 22   Moon Sign Cancer

am . . . .

pm . . . .
What really sets you apart at the moment is your huge and all-
encompassing heart. You can use this to help out anyone who is in
trouble or who needs timely advice. It might be suggested that Gemini
is much better at sorting out the lives of others than it is at dealing with
its own.

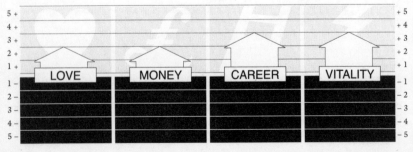

12 MONDAY   *Moon Age Day 23   Moon Sign Cancer*

am . . . .

pm . . . .
From a purely emotional point of view this interlude could be rather up
and down. The Moon is in your solar third house and this does at least
allow you the chance to verbalise your deeper feelings. Getting to grips
with a colleague or friend who has let you down badly in the recent past
could prove to be easier than you thought.

13 TUESDAY   *Moon Age Day 24   Moon Sign Leo*

am . . . .

pm . . . .
If you keep yourself busy today, you may not have quite as much time to
spend counselling others as both they and you might wish. All the same
it's worth finding a few moments to look after the interests of family
members, and to show them that their needs and concerns are well
understood.

14 WEDNESDAY   *Moon Age Day 25   Moon Sign Leo*

am . . . .

pm . . . .
Affairs of the heart are well accented under present trends, assisting you
to make the sort of first impression for which Gemini is famous. Whoever
you encounter today, it will be possible for you to weigh up the pros and
cons of their nature and to react accordingly. Sporting matters are also
highlighted.

15 THURSDAY   *Moon Age Day 26   Moon Sign Virgo*

am . . . .

pm . . . .
There are better times on offer when it comes to getting on well at work.
Some Gemini subjects might be thinking about a total change of career
but this may turn out to be unnecessary. The one thing you don't need
this month is to become bored with your lot in life. Why not find some
way to bring more excitement to your daily routines?

16 FRIDAY
Moon Age Day 27   Moon Sign Virgo

am . . . .

pm . . . .
Some extra care would be wise over decisions at work, though in a social sense you have scope to push ahead progressively and make a good impression on almost anyone you meet. The result could be a series of new friends or an association with a group that hasn't played an important part in your life up to now.

17 SATURDAY
Moon Age Day 28   Moon Sign Libra

am . . . .

pm . . . .
If it comes to a heated discussion or even a row, your position is assisted by Mars in your solar third house. This planetary position strengthens your powers of persuasion but it can also encourage you to defend yourself before you have been attacked. It would be easy to upset people.

18 SUNDAY
Moon Age Day 0   Moon Sign Libra

am . . . .

pm . . . .
Trends suggest you won't want to do anything that goes against the grain today and may be quite happy to simply potter about in a way that suits you. That's fine as far as it goes but it doesn't take account of necessary responsibilities and the needs of family members. Beware of being far too casual and inclined to shrug things off.

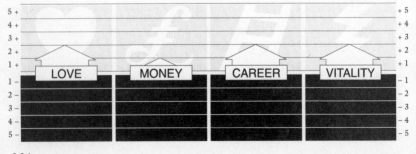

19 MONDAY

Moon Age Day 1   Moon Sign Scorpio

am . . . .

pm . . . .
Your commitment to work is noteworthy as long as things are going your way, but you may not take kindly to anyone telling you how things should be done. Once again that third-house Mars encourages you to put people in their place immediately if you sense that they are about to find any sort of fault with you.

20 TUESDAY

Moon Age Day 2   Moon Sign Scorpio

am . . . .

pm . . . .
Now is the time to look carefully at your finances and make any minor adjustments that seem necessary. For today you have scope to remain active and enterprising, but changes are on the way and you should avoid taking on too much for tomorrow and Thursday. Don't be afraid to put a full stop to some issues right now.

21 WEDNESDAY

Moon Age Day 3   Moon Sign Sagittarius

am . . . .

pm . . . .
Rather than pursuing new challenges now, you may be happiest when you can simply plod along at your own chosen pace. The lunar low emphasies your emotional response and you could feel as if there is nothing ahead that appears exciting. Don't react too strongly to what is a minor blip and nothing more.

22 THURSDAY

Moon Age Day 4   Moon Sign Sagittarius

am . . . .

pm . . . .
Chances are you will still not be giving of your best or feeling as though life is the sort of cornucopia you expect it to be. As a result you could be moody and inclined to show a sort of pessimism that is contrary to your usual nature. Very soon indeed the clouds will clear and you can bring an entirely different approach to the weekend.

23 FRIDAY

Moon Age Day 5   Moon Sign Sagittarius

am . . . .

pm . . . .
Although you may start out today in very much the same frame of mind that has predominated for a couple of days, it shouldn't be long before you are taking an interest again and are willing to pursue new topics and a host of different tasks. Be prepared to let friends bring you out of yourself at this time.

24 SATURDAY

Moon Age Day 6   Moon Sign Capricorn

am . . . .

pm . . . .
The weekend positively demands that you have fun and that you take other people with you on the roller coaster ride that is the Gemini life. You have what it takes to get them to join in, and there ought to be many laughs today. In terms of your social and romantic life you appear to be able to sort things out.

25 SUNDAY

Moon Age Day 7   Moon Sign Capricorn

am . . . .

pm . . . .
The Moon is in your solar eighth house, supporting a change in the way you approach deeper relationships. Perhaps you have been rather too serious or have looked on the downside of things for a while. For whatever reason, the time is right for a lighter touch and for showing a greater willingness to share in just about everything.

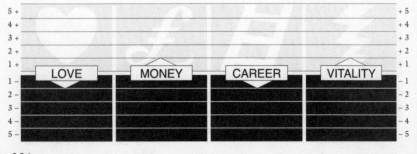

26 MONDAY
Moon Age Day 8   Moon Sign Aquarius

am . . . .

pm . . . .
A full commitment to either career or education enables you to learn quickly, adapt instantly and make the best of impressions on just about anyone. It will still be necessary to do the things you don't want to do first, before you embark upon more enjoyable pursuits. Start early in the day and then you should have plenty of time for everything.

27 TUESDAY
Moon Age Day 9   Moon Sign Aquarius

am . . . .

pm . . . .
An even-handed approach to the opinions of your friends is vital if you don't want to give unintended offence. Trends now encourage you to adapt yourself to the views of others. Just bear in mind that even you can be quite difficult on rare occasions. Everyone has their off days.

28 WEDNESDAY
Moon Age Day 10   Moon Sign Aquarius

am . . . .

pm . . . .
You are potentially very responsive to the changing positions of the Moon this month and might get on especially well with people who are ruled by that heavenly body. This means you should look out for people born under the zodiac sign of Cancer the Crab. Such individuals may have something to offer you that could turn out to be fantastic.

29 THURSDAY
Moon Age Day 11   Moon Sign Pisces

am . . . .

pm . . . .
With your ruling planet Mercury now in your solar sixth house you have what it takes to be even-handed, fair and not too discriminating. Under most circumstances you are totally ignorant of class or background, and all manner of people might be playing an important part in your life for the remainder of this month and into the next.

30 FRIDAY
Moon Age Day 12   Moon Sign Pisces

am . . . .

pm . . . .
You can now be an inspiration to others and show by your attitudes and actions that you are a worthy role model. Do your best to avoid family arguments or even disputes with friends because once you start arguing now it may be difficult for you to stop. Even if not everything goes your way on this particular Friday, the horizon looks good.

31 SATURDAY
Moon Age Day 13   Moon Sign Aries

am . . . .

pm . . . .
Make the most of a weekend that offers significant chance for diversity – which of course is what you seek more than anything else. You will be quite energetic and willing to join in with group situations. Gemini loves to be ahead of the field as a rule but this tendency is much less emphasised for the next couple of days.

1 SUNDAY
Moon Age Day 14   Moon Sign Aries

am . . . .

pm . . . .
Trends assist you to get yourself noticed through the things you do for others. You can also increase your popularity, and use this to attract social invitations. Even if you fancy a rest, that can come later. For the moment, just enjoy yourself.

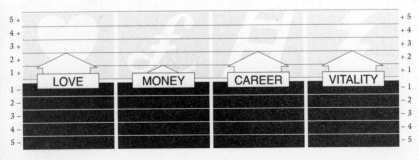

♏ ♊ November
2009

YOUR MONTH AT A GLANCE

⊕ = Opportunities are around   ⊖ = Be on the defensive   = Life is pretty ordinary

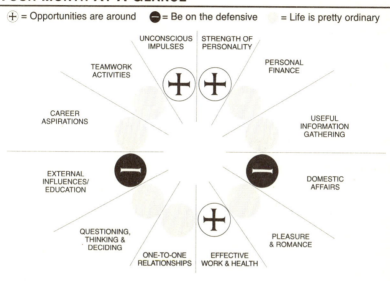

- UNCONSCIOUS IMPULSES — ⊕
- STRENGTH OF PERSONALITY — ⊕
- PERSONAL FINANCE
- TEAMWORK ACTIVITIES
- CAREER ASPIRATIONS
- USEFUL INFORMATION GATHERING
- EXTERNAL INFLUENCES/ EDUCATION — ⊖
- DOMESTIC AFFAIRS — ⊖
- QUESTIONING, THINKING & DECIDING
- ONE-TO-ONE RELATIONSHIPS
- EFFECTIVE WORK & HEALTH — ⊕
- PLEASURE & ROMANCE

NOVEMBER HIGHS AND LOWS

Here I show you how the rhythms of the Moon will affect you this month. Like the tide, your energies and abilities will rise and fall with its pattern. When it is above the centre line, go for it, when it is below, you should be resting.

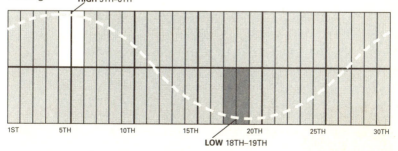

HIGH 5TH–6TH

1ST   5TH   10TH   15TH   20TH   25TH   30TH

LOW 18TH–19TH

2 MONDAY
Moon Age Day 15   Moon Sign Aries

am . . . .

pm . . . .
You have what it takes to move mountains today, but beware of getting too involved in case there are more obstacles and less success tomorrow. This is a week of two halves because although slightly quieter times are in store, by Thursday you should be pushing as hard as you can. Try to iron out the ups and downs of life this week.

3 TUESDAY
Moon Age Day 16   Moon Sign Taurus

am . . . .

pm . . . .
What sets today apart? Well, your sensitivity and emotions are to the fore, particularly in response to the problems of others. You might even feel bad about something that is happening at the other side of the world, but fortunately such trends don't last long for Gemini.

4 WEDNESDAY
Moon Age Day 17   Moon Sign Taurus

am . . . .

pm . . . .
Slowly but surely the mist is clearing, allowing you to see the potential future in stark contrast. If there isn't much you can do about ordering events today, a little patience would be best. A day to clear the decks for action because there are positive times ahead and the lunar high is going to offer you better and better prospects.

5 THURSDAY
Moon Age Day 18   Moon Sign Gemini

am . . . .

pm . . . .
The lunar high is going to be extremely potent this time round and offers you the sort of incentives that really enliven the Gemini life. Be prepared to be out there doing everything possible to advance your lot and persuading others to lend their support. You have what it takes to impress numerous people this week.

6 FRIDAY
Moon Age Day 19   Moon Sign Gemini

am . . . .

pm . . . .
This is the best time of the month for moving forward in your career and for showing others just how capable you can be. If anyone ever doubted your abilities when it comes to talking, make sure they can't do so at present. A little luck is available, assisting you to pick out the winners much easier than you might as a rule.

7 SATURDAY
Moon Age Day 20   Moon Sign Cancer

am . . . .

pm . . . .
With the weekend comes a chance to get things sorted out at home. DIY enthusiasts might decide to tear down walls, build new ones or redecorate. There is a strong 'spring-clean' feeling about, which though odd for this time of year can help you to feel better and act more spontaneously.

8 SUNDAY
Moon Age Day 21   Moon Sign Cancer

am . . . .

pm . . . .
Don't put off until another time what you can quite easily achieve now. Even if there are all sorts of possible diversions around, there are jobs that need finishing and that has to come first. If you put down your tools now it will be more difficult to pick them up later, and you may also go down in the estimation of loved ones.

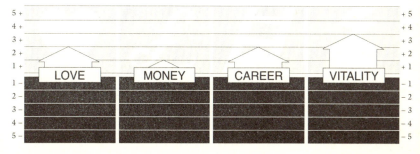

9 MONDAY

Moon Age Day 22   Moon Sign Leo

am . . . .

pm . . . .
A favourable time to heap all the love and devotion you can muster upon someone who is very special to you. Those little things that make all the difference come as second nature to you at the moment, and making someone really happy is more or less what your life is about today. Try to smooth out any disagreements at home.

10 TUESDAY

Moon Age Day 23   Moon Sign Leo

am . . . .

pm . . . .
The Sun in your sixth house enhances your exuberant and outgoing side – not that there is anything especially unusual about this for Gemini. You can best avoid getting into a muddle at work by seeking out people who can lend you a timely hand. No reasonable request is likely to be denied you.

11 WEDNESDAY

Moon Age Day 24   Moon Sign Virgo

am . . . .

pm . . . .
Trends highlight your desire to have things just so, and especially so when it comes to your home environment. 'A place for everything and everything in its place' is hardly your usual adage but seems to be so under present planetary influences. This might surprise those with whom you live and can also be a cause of no small amusement.

12 THURSDAY

Moon Age Day 25   Moon Sign Virgo

am . . . .

pm . . . .
Your strength lies in your ability to take challenges at work in your stride and actually enjoy the cut and thrust of a fairly demanding interlude. In the main you should be on top form and more than willing to take on even more adventures once the demands of the working day are out of the way.

13 FRIDAY
Moon Age Day 26   Moon Sign Libra

am . . . .

pm . . . .
OK, so it's Friday the thirteenth, but that doesn't mean that things are necessarily going wrong in your case. On the contrary, you can make this a more than usually successful sort of day and one during which there is great entertainment on offer. You could certainly spend a large proportion of the day with a smile on your face.

14 SATURDAY
Moon Age Day 27   Moon Sign Libra

am . . . .

pm . . . .
When it comes to the needs of relatives and friends you can afford to be quite outspoken today and you may not take kindly to seeing anyone used or put upon. Gemini now decides that it has the solutions to the world's problems and will set out to put things right. That's fine in principle, but slightly more difficult in practice.

15 SUNDAY
Moon Age Day 28   Moon Sign Scorpio

am . . . .

pm . . . .
Be prepared to become one of life's grazers today because there is nothing in particular that takes your fancy or attention but rather a wide cross-section of possibilities. Why not catch up on reading matter and make sure that all communications are well up to date? Other than that, don't be afraid to relax!

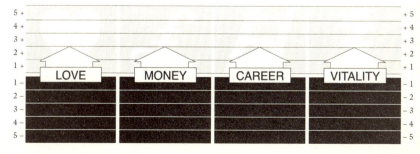

16 MONDAY

Moon Age Day 29   Moon Sign Scorpio

am . . . .

pm . . . .
As far as work is concerned, you can get difficult jobs done in a moment, whilst impossible ones could take a little longer. There could hardly be a better set of planetary circumstances when it comes to getting on well in life, though don't expect these trends to be with you throughout the whole week, because there are hiccups.

17 TUESDAY

Moon Age Day 0   Moon Sign Scorpio

am . . . .

pm . . . .
You have what it takes to keep things running well and to seek out increased responsibility. That's fine for today but by tomorrow you could be slowing down somewhat. It might be best to pace yourself, both in work and out of it.

18 WEDNESDAY

Moon Age Day 1   Moon Sign Sagittarius

am . . . .

pm . . . .
The more relaxed your attitude is, the better today is likely to work out for you. In an ideal world you will take a break from the major tasks and simply coast along for a day or two. If you manage this almost impossible feat, the lunar low could pass without notice. Far more likely is that you will try to plough on at full speed.

19 THURSDAY

Moon Age Day 2   Moon Sign Sagittarius

am . . . .

pm . . . .
Now is the time you should realise that even Gemini has its limitations. It would be very easy to get yourself into a mess and to make mistakes from the moment you get up until the time you climb back into bed. If you are steady and circumspect the day will work well for you, though both compliments and major success may be hard to find.

20 FRIDAY
Moon Age Day 3   Moon Sign Capricorn

am . . . .

pm . . . .
The lunar low is now out of the way and you can resume your accustomed course through life. Even if you are fairly happy with your lot, there might be one or two problems caused by people who seem unwilling to do what is expected of them. A little persuasion may be necessary and a forthright attitude if that doesn't work.

21 SATURDAY
Moon Age Day 4   Moon Sign Capricorn

am . . . .

pm . . . .
With some effort on your part you can reach destinations that seemed barred to you only a week or two ago. The change is in your ability to influence those around you, some of whom are now much more willing to let you have your way. Don't get involved in arguments that have nothing whatsoever to do with you.

22 SUNDAY
Moon Age Day 5   Moon Sign Capricorn

am . . . .

pm . . . .
Co-operating with others makes life go with a swing, and since you are generally quite flexible in your attitude this is no hardship for you. You can make this a Sunday of interest and originality, with plenty to set it apart from the routine. An ideal time to tackle tasks that come along in advance of the winter.

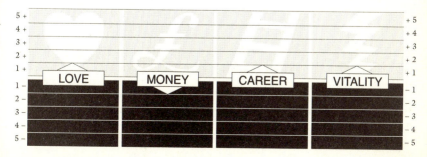

23 MONDAY   *Moon Age Day 6   Moon Sign Aquarius*

am . . . .

pm . . . .
As a new week dawns you could be plagued by small problems that you
have had no part in creating but which you will be expected to sort out.
If people can heap their own responsibilities on your shoulders they may
well do so at the moment. Your best response is to make it plain that you
will help if you can but can't be held responsible.

24 TUESDAY   *Moon Age Day 7   Moon Sign Aquarius*

am . . . .

pm . . . .
Look to what is necessary today and leave other matters until another
day. If you plan your hours sensibly you can get through a mountain of
jobs, whilst at the same time being relaxed and enjoying the ride.
Capitalise on the fact that people tend to come good when it matters the
most and on new social possibilities for the colder months.

25 WEDNESDAY   *Moon Age Day 8   Moon Sign Pisces*

am . . . .

pm . . . .
With one eye on the past and the other on the future you are able to learn
from what you did before and to modify your stance when it is necessary.
You have scope to make financial gains, even if these are small in size.
What really matters is that you can make progress towards longer-term
objectives.

26 THURSDAY   *Moon Age Day 9   Moon Sign Pisces*

am . . . .

pm . . . .
The more you throw in your lot with others during this part of the week,
the greater are the rewards that you can achieve. It is true that you have
to pay full attention at the moment and that you may not have quite the
level of personal success you would wish, but there is a good chance you
are achieving more than you think.

27 FRIDAY

Moon Age Day 10   Moon Sign Pisces

am . . . .

pm . . . .
The Sun now in your solar seventh house encourages a slightly ambivalent attitude to life and your mind may not be quite as focused as would sometimes be the case. More meditation is the key, together with listening to your unconscious thoughts. Intuition is growing in intensity.

28 SATURDAY

Moon Age Day 11   Moon Sign Aries

am . . . .

pm . . . .
Go slowly today – not because there is any lack of energy or potential success but simply because Gemini is inclined to rush its fences and to fall occasionally as a result. The more circumspect you manage to be, the better is the chance that things will go your way. This is a weekend of opportunity and one that can offer fun too.

29 SUNDAY

Moon Age Day 12   Moon Sign Aries

am . . . .

pm . . . .
In the sphere of romance you are now at your very best and you shouldn't have to do a great deal in order to get others to love you. On the contrary, you could be rather embarrassed by the amount of attention that you are attracting from specific directions. It's worth making your position clear in order to avoid jealousy.

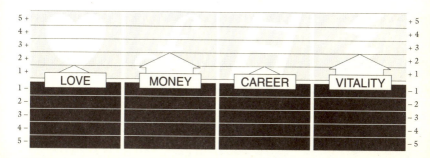

30 MONDAY   *Moon Age Day 13   Moon Sign Taurus*

am . . . .

pm . . . .
As the Moon takes a journey into your solar twelfth house, this has
potential to be the slowest start to a new week for quite some time. A
couple of days lie ahead of you during which you can afford to do more
planning than acting, though you can benefit from intervention from
people who are definitely seeing things your way.

1 TUESDAY   *Moon Age Day 14   Moon Sign Taurus*

am . . . .

pm . . . .
Another fairly steady sort of day introduces you to December and you
may also have the time to realise just how close Christmas is getting. Now
is the time to get your head round what to buy for those people who
always seem so difficult to please – though in fact you probably please
them all the time. Prepare yourself for action tomorrow.

2 WEDNESDAY   *Moon Age Day 15   Moon Sign Gemini*

am . . . .

pm . . . .
The lunar high has arrived and this is going to be potentially one of the
most hectic days in December. This is especially true if you are trying to
get everything done at the same time and capitalising on your level of
good luck. All the same a couple of genuine successes are all it takes to
make today special.

3 THURSDAY   *Moon Age Day 16   Moon Sign Gemini*

am . . . .

pm . . . .
Make the most of possibilities that come your way out of the blue. There
is nobody in the length and breadth of the zodiac that can take advantage
of changing times in the way you can, and the lunar high offers plenty.
You might have to refuse a social invitation, simply on the grounds that
you can't be in two places at once.

4 FRIDAY

Moon Age Day 17   Moon Sign Cancer

am . . . .

pm . . . .
You remain on a roll, even though the lunar high has now passed. The
fact is that you still want to have the penny and the bun in all possible
cases. Of course this won't be the case but if you can even get halfway to
some of your objectives you will be doing extremely well. A day to give
a definite boost to your personal popularity.

5 SATURDAY

Moon Age Day 18   Moon Sign Cancer

am . . . .

pm . . . .
Not every area of your life is equally productive at this time and you will
need to be fairly careful about what you take on this weekend. Personal
annoyance could come in your case from chasing a dream miles along the
road, only to find it disappearing before your eyes. It's better to play for
certainties than to indulge in pipe dreams.

6 SUNDAY

Moon Age Day 19   Moon Sign Leo

am . . . .

pm . . . .
Trends suggest that there is much to take your attention and a great deal
of planning to do. With Christmas in view you may be getting out strings
of lights, but do be careful on that wonky ladder. It isn't that you are
accident-prone today, but all the same, Gemini is inclined to chance its
arm too much on occasions. Enlist some practical support.

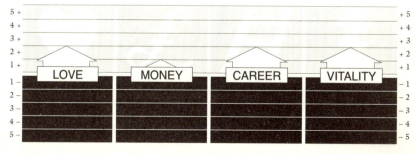

149

December

2009

YOUR MONTH AT A GLANCE

⊕ = Opportunities are around   ⊖ = Be on the defensive   ⬤ = Life is pretty ordinary

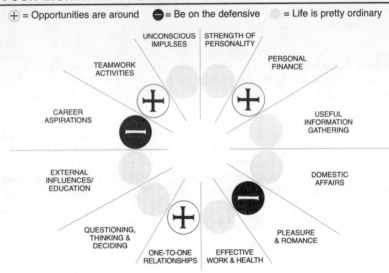

UNCONSCIOUS IMPULSES

STRENGTH OF PERSONALITY

TEAMWORK ACTIVITIES

PERSONAL FINANCE

CAREER ASPIRATIONS

USEFUL INFORMATION GATHERING

EXTERNAL INFLUENCES/ EDUCATION

DOMESTIC AFFAIRS

QUESTIONING, THINKING & DECIDING

PLEASURE & ROMANCE

ONE-TO-ONE RELATIONSHIPS

EFFECTIVE WORK & HEALTH

DECEMBER HIGHS AND LOWS

Here I show you how the rhythms of the Moon will affect you this month. Like the tide, your energies and abilities will rise and fall with its pattern. When it is above the centre line, go for it, when it is below, you should be resting. **HIGH** 2ND–3RD

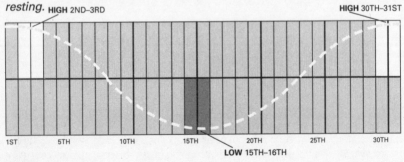

HIGH 30TH–31ST

1ST   5TH   10TH   15TH   20TH   25TH   30TH

LOW 15TH–16TH

7 MONDAY
Moon Age Day 20   Moon Sign Leo

am . . . .

pm . . . .
You know what you want to say today and shouldn't have any difficulty at all getting your message across to others. The only slight fly in the ointment is that you could be rather too direct for some people and that could lead to arguments. There are times when you need to be somewhat more diplomatic and to show sensitivity.

8 TUESDAY
Moon Age Day 21   Moon Sign Virgo

am . . . .

pm . . . .
You can afford to turn your mind and your actions in the direction of those you love today. Even if you retain your ability to get things right first time at work, the needs and wants of your relatives could well take up more of your time generally. Splitting your day could be problematical, but is possible all the same.

9 WEDNESDAY
Moon Age Day 22   Moon Sign Virgo

am . . . .

pm . . . .
The position of the Sun in your chart assists in your efforts to get most things right first time. This is because you can be quite exacting in your actions and thoughtful about consequences. You may get stuck on occasions, but can obtain the right sort of advice from people around you.

10 THURSDAY
Moon Age Day 23   Moon Sign Libra

am . . . .

pm . . . .
The focus moves away from creature comforts, allowing you to ignore any need for greater security or forward planning. On the contrary, you have what it takes to make up your mind instantly and to think much more about what is happening around you now. In more than one way you have scope to forge ahead.

11 FRIDAY
Moon Age Day 24   Moon Sign Libra

am . . . .

pm . . . .
From an emotional viewpoint you could be hanging on to issues and situations from the past that have little or nothing to do with your life at the moment. This is in sharp contrast to your more practical mind, which is proceeding without any interruption or delay. Two opposing attitudes at the same time might be somewhat confusing.

12 SATURDAY
Moon Age Day 25   Moon Sign Libra

am . . . .

pm . . . .
There are signs that decisions are still being made instantly and without too much recourse to the opinions of other people. It isn't that you are insensitive – merely that you are sure of your position and you remain certain that what is good for you will help those around you. That might well be true, but it's worth explaining the fact to them.

13 SUNDAY
Moon Age Day 26   Moon Sign Scorpio

am . . . .

pm . . . .
In the main you are a leader and not a follower. This tendency is much enhanced at present, and you could easily fall out with anyone who tries to insist that you follow any course of action that is not inspired from within yourself. You need to be in command, and this is the fact that has potential to cause you a few upsets around now.

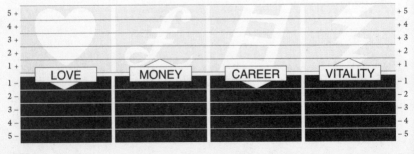

14 MONDAY

Moon Age Day 27   Moon Sign Scorpio

am . . . .

pm . . . .
Today should be slightly better when it comes to your poise and balance. Now is the time to gradually begin to take others into consideration, not simply in your mind but verbally too. The strange thing is that once you do explain yourself practically everyone will fall in line. It's not what you do that counts but how you go about it.

15 TUESDAY

Moon Age Day 28   Moon Sign Sagittarius

am . . . .

pm . . . .
With the lunar low around you can't expect to keep up the same pace that has been possible across the last few days. Instead of trying to get everything sorted out yourself it's worth relying on colleagues and friends. Plans for Christmas might be subject to slight setbacks, but you can sort these out ahead of the day.

16 WEDNESDAY

Moon Age Day 0   Moon Sign Sagittarius

am . . . .

pm . . . .
This is no time to gamble wildly on things turning out well simply because you want them to. What is required while the Sun is in Sagittarius is better planning and a few trial runs. Even if you can gain support from most people, some may take more persuading than usual.

17 THURSDAY

Moon Age Day 1   Moon Sign Capricorn

am . . . .

pm . . . .
It's worth being up and about early today, getting yourself right back on form and making the most of the day. The Moon has moved on and now you respond more to better planetary trends. At last you can get your head round what you plan to do for Christmas – probably much to the relief of your loved ones.

18 FRIDAY
Moon Age Day 2   Moon Sign Capricorn

am . . . .

pm . . . .
There are possible gains to be made today on account of your quick thinking and your desire to act on impulse. This isn't always the case of course, but for the moment you can get people to fall in line with your thinking and to support you. Too many rules and regulations may well get on your nerves at times like this.

19 SATURDAY
Moon Age Day 3   Moon Sign Capricorn

am . . . .

pm . . . .
Find the right people today – that is the most important advice whilst the Sun occupies its present position in your solar chart. It doesn't matter whether you need the chimney sweeping or if you want to organise a trip somewhere. There is always someone around who is an expert, and you need to find that individual now.

20 SUNDAY
Moon Age Day 4   Moon Sign Aquarius

am . . . .

pm . . . .
Some situations could seem irritating – even if the core of the problem is your own state of mind. You probably won't get everything you want simply by wishing it was so and extra effort will be necessary if you want to persuade others that you have all the answers. Be prepared to get to grips with social demands before things get too hectic.

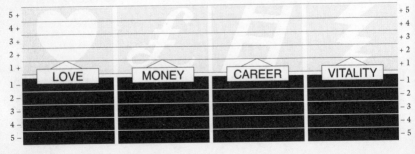

21 MONDAY
Moon Age Day 5   Moon Sign Aquarius

am . . . .

pm . . . .
If there is any tension about today you can do a great deal to dissipate it, merely by being your usual charming self. People love to have you around, particularly if you are good at entertaining them. You have scope to be increasingly on show for the next few days, not just because of Christmas but on account of changing planetary trends.

22 TUESDAY
Moon Age Day 6   Moon Sign Pisces

am . . . .

pm . . . .
Laughter is truly the best tonic at the moment and you can really take the heat out of almost any situation with your cheerful and joking attitude to life. There are some slight financial gains available, even if these are only a realisation that you are slightly better off than you thought. Confidence generally is beginning to grow.

23 WEDNESDAY
Moon Age Day 7   Moon Sign Pisces

am . . . .

pm . . . .
Just remember that even a Gemini cannot please all of the people all of the time. There may well be a few people around now who will remain dissatisfied with whatever you do. Instead of concentrating on the awkward types, why not look towards the multitude that think you are the bee's knees?

24 THURSDAY
Moon Age Day 8   Moon Sign Pisces

am . . . .

pm . . . .
Christmas Eve brings a change of position in the case of the Sun in your solar chart. With the Sun now in your eighth house you have what it takes to change things, even at the last minute. Just bear in mind that less progressive types will have the collywobbles if you suddenly announce that Christmas is in for a revolution!

25 FRIDAY

Moon Age Day 9   Moon Sign Aries

am . . . .

pm . . . .
You can afford to enjoy everything that Christmas Day has to offer in the knowledge that almost everyone around you is happy and contented. That may also include you, but under present trends there may still be things that seem too routine and inflexible. Curb your natural enthusiasm for upheaval, at least for a day or two.

26 SATURDAY

Moon Age Day 10   Moon Sign Aries

am . . . .

pm . . . .
Now would be a good time for travel, even if you are only thinking in terms of short journeys to visit relatives or friends. You probably won't want to stop at home throughout the whole Christmas period, and will get bored unless you ring the changes in some way. You become more and more a party animal as the days progress.

27 SUNDAY

Moon Age Day 11   Moon Sign Taurus

am . . . .

pm . . . .
Even if the pace of life refuses to slow down, you may decide to draw in your horns a little whilst the Moon is in your twelfth house. The focus is on spending more time with your lover, and devoting attention to family members. This would be a good time to get some fresh air and to fly a kite or to go walking.

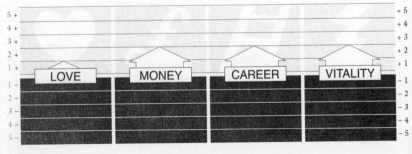

28 MONDAY
Moon Age Day 12   Moon Sign Taurus

am . . . .

pm . . . .
The start of a new week might go more or less unnoticed if you are not committed to work until after the New Year. For those around you it will be more of the same but you may well be bored with Christmas cake and social gatherings. The present position of the Sun encourages you to change something – possibly anything!

29 TUESDAY
Moon Age Day 13   Moon Sign Taurus

am . . . .

pm . . . .
Your strength lies in your ability to concentrate on your own inner thoughts. Emotions could run high in the family and whether you realise it or not some of them are being jacked up by your own present attitude. Listen to younger people especially today.

30 WEDNESDAY
Moon Age Day 14   Moon Sign Gemini

am . . . .

pm . . . .
What a way to end a year! The lunar high pays you a timely visit and helps you to speed up the pace of your life and your thinking. Now you should be quite happy to party with almost anyone and won't need a second invitation to be with your friends. The very best of what Gemini can be is likely to be on display both today and tomorrow.

31 THURSDAY
Moon Age Day 15   Moon Sign Gemini

am . . . .

pm . . . .
With tremendous energy and a smile on your face from morning until night you can definitely be the right person to be putting up those balloons ready for the big shindig. The very last thing you will want to do is to spend the last hours of the year in quiet contemplation. Wherever the action is, that is where you need to be.

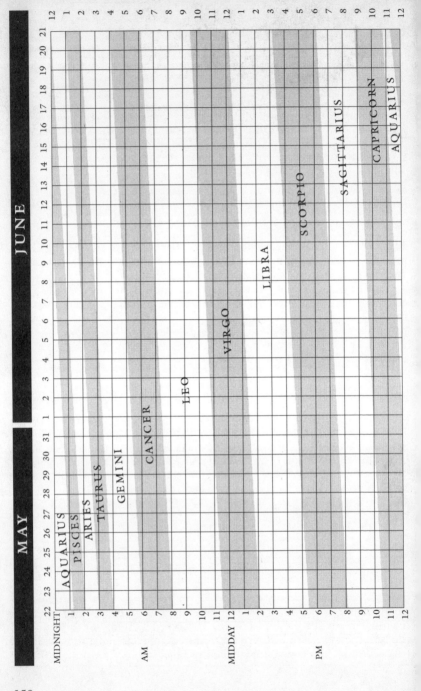

THE ZODIAC, PLANETS AND CORRESPONDENCES

The Earth revolves around the Sun once every calendar year, so when viewed from Earth the Sun appears in a different part of the sky as the year progresses. In astrology, these parts of the sky are divided into the signs of the zodiac and this means that the signs are organised in a circle. The circle begins with Aries and ends with Pisces.

Taking the zodiac sign as a starting point, astrologers then work with all the positions of planets, stars and many other factors to calculate horoscopes and birth charts and tell us what the stars have in store for us.

The table below shows the planets and Elements for each of the signs of the zodiac. Each sign belongs to one of the four Elements: Fire, Air, Earth or Water. Fire signs are creative and enthusiastic; Air signs are mentally active and thoughtful; Earth signs are constructive and practical; Water signs are emotional and have strong feelings.

It also shows the metals and gemstones associated with, or corresponding with, each sign. The correspondence is made when a metal or stone possesses properties that are held in common with a particular sign of the zodiac.

Finally, the table shows the opposite of each star sign – this is the opposite sign in the astrological circle.

Placed	Sign	Symbol	Element	Planet	Metal	Stone	Opposite
1	Aries	Ram	Fire	Mars	Iron	Bloodstone	Libra
2	Taurus	Bull	Earth	Venus	Copper	Sapphire	Scorpio
3	Gemini	Twins	Air	Mercury	Mercury	Tiger's Eye	Sagittarius
4	Cancer	Crab	Water	Moon	Silver	Pearl	Capricorn
5	Leo	Lion	Fire	Sun	Gold	Ruby	Aquarius
6	Virgo	Maiden	Earth	Mercury	Mercury	Sardonyx	Pisces
7	Libra	Scales	Air	Venus	Copper	Sapphire	Aries
8	Scorpio	Scorpion	Water	Pluto	Plutonium	Jasper	Taurus
9	Sagittarius	Archer	Fire	Jupiter	Tin	Topaz	Gemini
10	Capricorn	Goat	Earth	Saturn	Lead	Black Onyx	Cancer
11	Aquarius	Waterbearer	Air	Uranus	Uranium	Amethyst	Leo
12	Pisces	Fishes	Water	Neptune	Tin	Moonstone	Virgo

Foulsham books can be found in all
good bookshops or direct from
www.foulsham.com